PRACTICAL JAPANESE

3

JN090574

JLPT N3, N4 Grammar and Useful Expressions
JLPT N3, N4 レベルの基礎文法と使える表現

小川 清美＝著
Orrin Cummins＝英語監修

IBC パブリッシング

はじめに

　本書は、PRACTICAL JAPANESE 3 ということで、この PRACTICAL JAPANESE シリーズの3冊目であり、最後の本となります。この3冊を勉強することで、文法の基礎：形容詞と動詞の活用、接続詞を、ほぼすべて習得することができます。これは、JLPT（日本語能力試験）では、N4からN3のレベルに値します。このN4からN3レベルというのは、日常会話ができるレベルと設定されているので、この本を学習し終えるころには、日本人との会話が自由にできるようになるはずです。

　さらに、本書には、友達と話す時のくだけた表現から、会社や近所の人と話すときの丁寧な表現、さらにホテルやレストラン等で耳にする敬語まで、より日常で使えるような表現を取り入れました。

　私は執筆の傍らレッスンも行っており、日々生徒から色々な質問を受けます。その中でもよく聞かれるものを取りあげて、本書の最後に紹介しています。

　日本語を学んでいる皆さんにとって、日本語がぺらぺらになりたい、大好きな日本のドラマやアニメがわかるようになりたい、という目標は遠く感じることでしょう。しかし、ここで学んだ基礎をもとに、さらに様々な語彙や表現、日本語のニュアンスなどを学ぶことで、その目標に近づくことができるはずです。

　皆さんの目標到達のために本書が役に立つことを願います。

小川 清美

Preface

This is the third and final book of the Practical Japanese series. By studying the information in these three books, you can learn almost all the basics of Japanese grammar, from using adjectives and verbs to connecting phrases with conjunctions. This will put you somewhere between the N4 and N3 levels of the JLPT. And since that level of proficiency is designed to represent the ability to carry on daily conversations, you should be able to freely converse with Japanese people upon completing this book.

In this book, I've also included expressions that you will have many opportunities to use in everyday life, including casual phrases for chatting with friends, polite expressions for speaking with people at work or in the neighborhood, and even the honorific speech heard at places like hotels and restaurants.

I teach in addition to writing, so I hear a lot of different questions from students every day. At the end of this book you will find a selection of the most common queries.

I'm sure most Japanese learners feel that their goal of speaking the language fluently or understanding the dialogue of their favorite anime or drama is far away. But by studying new vocabulary words, expressions, and shades of nuance based on the fundamentals you learn in the Practical Japanese series, I have no doubt that you will draw nearer to the finish line.

I sincerely hope that this book will be useful in the pursuit of your goals.

Kiyomi Ogawa

Contents

Chapter 2 Various Expressions   69
第２章　いろいろな表現

Chapter 3 Conjunctions and Adverbs 97
第<ruby>3<rt></rt></ruby>章<ruby>だいさんしょう<rt></rt></ruby>　接続詞<ruby>せつぞくし<rt></rt></ruby>と副詞<ruby>ふくし<rt></rt></ruby>

How to Use This Book

In **Chapter 1**, we will study the usage of verbs.
First, try to memorize the different conjugated forms.

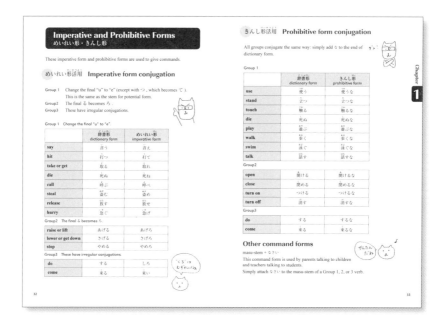

Review the main points and examples, then study how to use the verbs in sentences. This will help you understand the different ways they can be used.

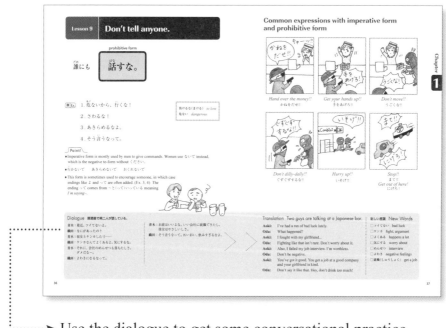

╌╌╌╌►Use the dialogue to get some conversational practice.

In **Chapter 2**, we will examine a variety of expressions while applying the grammatical rules we have learned thus far.

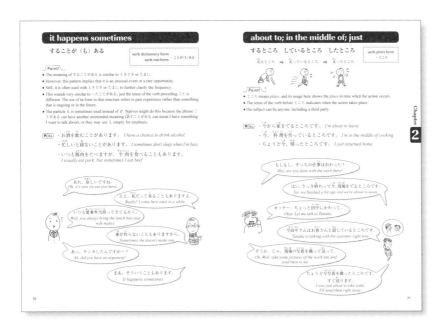

In **Chapter 3**, we will look at example sentences that contain adverbs, conjunctions, and other parts of speech. You can skip around this chapter and read the parts that most interest you first, if you want.

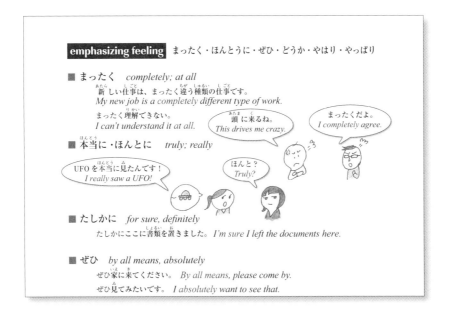

Various response and Useful phrases

Japanese people respond often during conversations to show that they are paying attention.

Agreement

えぇ／そう
formal informal

Disagreement

いえ／いや
formal informal

People often repeat these.
Ex. そうそう いえいえ

Surprised

ええっ!? わああ
What!?

Impressed

へえ〜 ほ〜
Oh? Hm

Thinking of what to say

えっと〜／ええと
Uhh... / Uhh

あの〜
Um...

Reactions

そうなんですか？／そうなの？／ほんと？
formal   informal   informal
Really?

そうですか／そっか
formal   informal
Oh, I see.

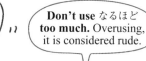

なるほど *Oh, I see.*
(I'm starting to understand.)

Don't use なるほど **too much.** Overusing, it is considered rude.

たいへんですね。
Sorry to hear that.

えらいですね。
You are great.

よかったですね。
That's good for you.

ぜんぜんだいじょうぶです。
informal
No problem at all.

ぜんぜんだいじょうぶ: technically incorrect, but used often

とんでもないです。
formal
No problem at all.

Slang you might hear a lot

やばい！
wow / oh no!

ちょう
super

めっちゃ
very

まじ？
Seriously?

ていうか
I mean

Useful phrases

別々にお願いします。
Separately, please.

袋 はいりません。
I don't need a plastic bag.

返品できますか？
Can I return this?

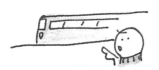

この電車は──に行きますか？
Does this train go to ──?

何番線ですか？
Which platform is it ?

──で乗り換えです。
transfer at──.

切符を間違えました。
I got the wrong ticket.

電車に忘れ物をしました。
I left something in the train.

Chapter 1

Verbs in Sentences

だいいっしょう　　　　　　　　　どうしぶん
第1章　さまざまな動詞文

Give / Receive あげる・くれる・もらう

There are two verbs that mean *to give*: あげる and くれる. They belong to Group 2. もらう means *to receive* and is in Group 1.

	辞書形	ない形	ます形	て形	た形
give	あげる	あげない	あげます	あげて	あげた
give me	くれる	くれない	くれます	くれて	くれた
receive	もらう	もらわない	もらいます	もらって	もらった

くれる is used when the recipient is you or someone close to you (socially, not physically). This is known as 身内. It includes your family members and other people within your social circle.

Sentence Structure

1. My teacher gave me [my little sister] a book.

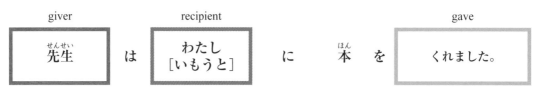

2. My teacher [I] gave that girl a book.

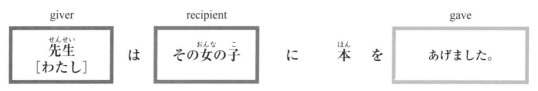

3. That girl [I] received a book from my teacher.

てあげる・てくれる・てもらう

When the thing being given or received is an action rather than an item, the te-form of the verb comes before it.

4. My teacher lent me [my little sister] a book.

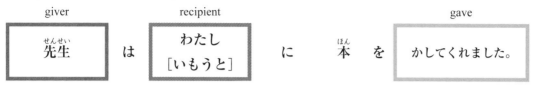

5. My teacher [I] lent that girl a book.

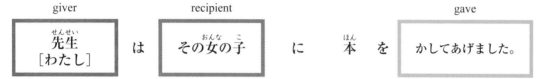

6. My friend [I] had my teacher lend her [me] a book.

Sentence Structure

When the direct object is a person, be careful which particle you use after it.
Indirect objects take に or から as seen above, but direct objects take を.

7. My teacher helped me [my little sister].

8. My teacher [I] helped that girl.

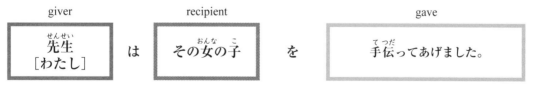

9. My friend [I] got my teacher to help him [me].

My teacher gave me a book.

giver　は / が　recipient　に　　　　gave

| 先生
せんせい | は | 私
わたし | に | 本
ほん | を | くれました。 |

例 Ex.

1. おばあちゃんはいつもお菓子
か し をくれる。

2. 友達
ともだち が 弟
おとうと にゲームをくれた。

3. 先生
せんせい は漢字
かん じ を教
おし えてくれる。

4. 塩
しお をとってくれますか？

おばあちゃん　*grandma*

ゲーム　*videogame*

塩　*salt*

とって《とる》　*to get, to pass*

Point!

- くれる is used when the recipient of the action is the speaker（私
わたし）or someone in the speaker's family or social circle (身内
み うち , see page 14).
- If the recipient is omitted from the sentence, then you know that it is 私
わたし because くれる indicates that (Ex. 1).
- If the giver is providing an action rather than an item, use te-form verbs ＋ くれる (Ex. 3).
- You can also use くれる for request, with a meaning equivalant to "Could you ...?" in English (Ex. 4).

Dialogue　アンは日本人の同僚、ゆかと話している。

ゆか：アンさん、よかったら、このペアのワイング
　　　ラス使ってくれますか？
　　　ともだちが結婚いわいにくれたんだけど、使
　　　わないから。

アン：え？ ほしいものじゃなかったんですか？
　　　私が結婚したとき、みんなが私たちのほしい
　　　物をおくってくれました。

ゆか：どうやってほしいものがわかるんですか？

アン：アメリカでは、デパートでほしい物のリスト
　　　をつくります。
　　　ネットでみることもできますから、べんりで
　　　すよ。

ゆか：へえ～。おもしろいですね。そのサイト、み
　　　せてくれませんか？

What's the difference? する vs. してくれる

The dictionary form of a verb is neutral in that it simply shows that an action took place. 〜てくれる, on the other hand, expresses the recipient's gratitude or appreciation for the action.

先生は日本語を 私 に教える。
doesn't show appreciation

先生は日本語を教えてくれる。
shows appreciation

One more thing...

We learned in Practical Japanese 1 that you can use 〜てください to politely ask someone to do something. ください is a conjugation of くださる, the polite form of the verb くれる.

However, くれますか is more polite than ください because it is a question rather than a statement.

教えてくれる？　　　教えてください。　教えてくれますか？　教えてくださいますか？
　くれない？　　　　　　　　　　　　　くれませんか？　　くださいませんか？

with family or friends　　　**at school or work**　　　**on very formal occasions**

Translation Anne is talking to her Japanese co-worker, Yuka.

Yuka: Anne, can you use these wine glasses for me?

A friend of mine gave them to me as a wedding present, but I never use them.

Anne: Oh, you didn't want them? When I got married, everyone gave us the things we wanted.

Yuka: How did they know what you want?

Anne: In the US, we create a wedding registry at the department store.

You can even view it online, so it is quite convenient.

Yuka: Wow, that's interesting. Can you show me the website?

新しい言葉　New Words

- □ 結婚(けっこん)　wedding
- □ いわい　gift/celebration
- □ おくって《おくる》
　to send gifts

giver	は / が	recipient	に		gave
先生（せんせい）	は	友達（ともだち）	に 本（ほん） を		あげました。

例 Ex.

1. 私（わたし）は友達（ともだち）に誕生日（たんじょうび）プレゼントをあげた。

2. 先生（せんせい）は友達（ともだち）に漢字（かんじ）を教（おし）えてあげる。

3. 困（こま）っている人（ひと）をたすけてあげたい。

4. どこかにつれてってあげようか。

> 困っている人
> *a person in trouble*
> つれてって《つれていく》
> *take a person somewhere*

Point!

- The giver can be anyone, but the speaker (私（わたし）) can't be the recipient.

- Various meanings can be expressed by changing the form of あげる at the end, like with 〜たい and *want to* (Ex. 3).

- The te-form of the verb can also be used with ようか to offer to do something for someone (Ex. 4). This is quite casual, however, so 〜てあげる is generally used with friends or family. For more formal situations, use 〜ましょうか or さしあげる instead (see page 62).

Dialogue　カップルが話している。

彼氏：どこ行く？ きみの行きたいところにつれてってあげるよ。

彼女：ほんと？ うれしい！ じゃ横浜につれてってくれる？

彼氏：給料出たから、今日はなんでもおごってやるよ。

彼女：おごってくれるの？ ありがと〜。

彼女：あ〜おいしかった！ あ、シャツにソースついてるよ。
ふいてあげる。

What's the difference?　あげる vs. やる

While やる is traditionally used for kids, subordinates, and pets, recently more people use あげる for plants and pets because やる sounds a little rough.

花に水をやる
water the flowers

犬にえさをやる
feed the dog

ワーイ

弟にゲームをやった。
I gave my little brother a videogame.

Watch out!

You can't use あげる for the following expressions:

賞をあたえる
give a prize

アイデア・宿題を出す
give an idea / or homework

薬を出す
give medicine

どうぞ

かぜ(病気)を
うつす
*give a cold
(illness)*

Translation A couple are talking.

Boyfriend: Where do you wanna go? I'll take you anywhere you want.

Girlfriend: Really? I'm so happy! Well, will you take me to Yokohama?

Boyfriend: I got my paycheck, so I'll treat you to anything today.

Girlfriend: You'll treat me? Thanks~

Girlfriend: Ahh, that was delicious! Oh, you got some sauce on your shirt.

I'll wipe it off for you.

新しい言葉 New Words

☐ 横浜　Yokohama City

☐ 給料(きゅうりょう)　salary, paycheck

☐ おごって《おごる》　to treat someone

☐ ソース　sauce

☐ ふいて《ふく》　to wipe (off)

Lesson 3　I received a book from my teacher.

recipient　　　　giver　　　　　　　　　received

私 は 先生 に/から 本 を もらいました。
わたし　　せんせい　　　　　　　ほん

例 Ex.

1. 弟は父におこづかいをもらった。
おとうと ちち

2. 友達に引っ越しを手伝ってもらった。
ともだち ひ こ　　　て つだ

3. 実家からお米を送ってもらった。
じっか　　こめ おく

4. 袋を無料でもらえますか。
ふくろ むりょう

おこづかい　*allowance*
引っ越し　*moving*
実家　*parents' house*
袋　*plastic bag*

Point!

- When describing the action of giving, the verb you use（くれる or あげる）depends on the recipient. But with receiving, you use もらう no matter who the recipient is.

- The particle に or から is used to mark the giver. Usually に means *to*, but with this verb it means *from*.

- However, から is always used when the giver is a place or organization (Ex. 3).

- もらえる is the potential form (*can receive*).

Dialogue　亮介が病院の受付の女性と話している。

女性：こちらの用紙に名前と住所、電話番号を書いてもらえますか。

亮介：はい。あっ、すみません。まちがえました。もう1枚用紙もらえますか。

女性：はい、どうぞ。それと保険証をみせてもらえますか。

亮介：保険証ですか。あっ、わすれちゃった…ちょっと待ってください。
もしもし、お母さん？ ごめん、保険証もってきてくれる？

What's the difference?　～てもらう vs. ～てくれる

知(し)らない人(ひと)に手伝(てつだ)ってもらった。
知(し)らない人(ひと)が手伝(てつだ)ってくれた。

These two sentences have the same basic meaning: *A stranger helped me.*
While you can say either one, there is a slight difference in their nuance.

～てもらう implies that the recipient is asking for help, whereas ～てくれる focuses on the giver (the help is provided voluntarily).

But don't worry—even native speakers don't strictly adhere to this rule, so you can still use くれる for making requests.

One more thing...

いただきます is the polite form of もらいます. Although it is used by itself before starting a meal (similar to the French *bon appétit*), it can also be used when receiving gifts or actions.

Just as もらいます becomes もらえますか in a request, いただきます changes into いただけますか.

見(み)てもらえる?　*family or friends*	見(み)てもらえますか?　*at school or work*	見(み)ていただけますか?　*on very formal occasions*

Translation Ryousuke is talking to the receptionist at a clinic.

Receptionist : Could you write down your name, address, and phone number on this form?

Ryousuke: Yes. Oh, sorry. I made a mistake. Can I have another form?

Receptionist: Sure, here you go. And could you show me your insurance card?

Ryousuke: Insurance card? Oh, I forgot it... Just a second, please.

Mom? Sorry, can you bring me my insurance card?

新しい言葉　New Words

☐ 受付(うけつけ)　reception
☐ 用紙(ようし)　a form
☐ まちがえました《まちがえる》
　　　　to make a mistake
☐ 保険証(ほけんしょう)
　　(medical) insurance card

Conditional Forms (if/when)
条件形 <ruby>条件形<rt>じょうけんけい</rt></ruby> たら、えば、なら、と

There are four conditional forms, each of which has a slightly different usage and nuance.

1. えば **final letter of dictionary form becomes *eba*.**
   used to state a certainty (in the eyes of the speaker)

2. と **dictionary form + と**
   repeated things; hopes

3. なら **dictionary form + なら**
   specific situations, suggestions, or requests

4. たら **ta-form + ら   したら**
   Widely used, especially by people from western Japan.
   This also used for saying "*After X, then Y.*"

As the below chart demonstrates, the usages of えば, なら, and と are limited—but たら can be used in practically any situation.

	えば、と、なら	たら
If I drink, I will definitely get drunk.	飲めば必ず酔う。	飲んだら必ず酔う。
Whenever I drink, I always get drunk.	飲むといつも酔う。	飲んだらいつも酔う。
I hope I can drink.	飲めるといいな。	飲めたらいいな。
If you're going to drink, I recommend that bar.	飲むならあの店がいい。	飲んだったらあの店がいい。
When I drank, I got drunk.		飲んだら酔った。

えばの活用表

Group 1 Change the final sound to "e" and add ば.

	辞書形 dictionary form	条件形 conditional form
to laugh	笑う	笑えば
to hit	打つ	打てば
to run	走る	走れば
to call	呼ぶ	呼べば
to rest	休む	休めば
to bake or grill	焼く	焼けば
to stop, cancel	よす	よせば

Group 2 Change the final る to れば.

to sleep	寝る	寝れば
to open	開ける	開ければ

Group 3 Same as Group 2, change the final る to れば.

to do	する	すれば
to come	来る	来れば

Others

Negative verbs: Change the final い to ければ

　　ない ➡ なければ　　食べなければ　　言わなければ

i-adjectives: Change the final い to ければ (affirmative) or くなければ (negative)

　　い ➡ ければ　　大きければ　大きくなければ

na-adjectives/nouns: Add であれば (affirmative) or でなければ (negative)

　　名詞 ➡ 日本であれば　　好きであれば　　好きでなければ

Lesson 4 — When spring comes, the cherry blossom will bloom.

Verb *eba*

春<ruby>は<rt>る</rt></ruby>に　**なれば**　桜<ruby>さくら<rt></rt></ruby>が咲<ruby>さ<rt></rt></ruby>きます。

例 Ex.

1. このスイッチを押<ruby>お<rt></rt></ruby>せば、電気<ruby>でんき<rt></rt></ruby>がつきます。

2. たくさん勉強<ruby>べんきょう<rt></rt></ruby>すれば、合格<ruby>ごうかく<rt></rt></ruby>します。

3. 走<ruby>はし<rt></rt></ruby>れば間<ruby>ま<rt></rt></ruby>に合<ruby>あ<rt></rt></ruby>う。

4. どうすればいいですか。

押せば《おす》 *to press*
電気 *light*
合格 *pass (an exam)*
走れば《はしる》 *to run*
間に合う *to be in time*

Point!

- the final *u* of dictionary form becomes *eba*.
- A えば B: the speaker is certain that B will result if A happens.
- If ____, *it's a sure bet* (Ex. 2, 3)
- どうすればいいですか is an oft-used expression that means *What should I do?* (Ex. 4)

Dialogue　先生と生徒が話している。

先生：あと一週間で試験ですね。がんばりましょう。

生徒：はい、きんちょうします。特にリスニングは自信がないんです。
どうすればいいですか？

先生：そうですね。聞くだけじゃなく、シャドウイングするといいですよ。

生徒：でも、はやすぎます。

先生：練習すれば慣れますよ。がんばってください。

生徒：はい！

Common expressions

いけません *means that something won't go well*
なければいけません *is "must"*

がんばらなければいけません
If you don't work hard, it won't go well. ➡ You must work hard.

ちりもつもれば山^{やま}となる
Even dust piled together will become a mountain.
(a famous proverb)

One more thing...

You can use this えば for past event that you regret, the first part is えば or なければ
and the second part is past tense.

あの店^{みせ}に行けば、買^かえた。(後悔^{こうかい})
If I had gone to that store, I could
have bought it. (indicates regret)

行^いかなければよかった。
It would have been better
if I hadn't gone.

勉強^{べんきょう}すれば合格^{ごうかく}したのに。
I would have passed
if I had studied, but...

＊のに means though, but it can also indicate regret.

Translation A teacher and a student are talking.

Teacher : Your exam is in a week. Let's work on it together.
Student : Yes, I'm nervous. I especially don't have confidence in
my listening ability.
What should I do?
Teacher : Well, you should do shadowing too, not just listening.
Student : But, it is too fast…
Teacher : If you practice, you will get used to it. Do the best you
can.
Student : Okay!

新しい言葉 New Words

□試験(しけん) exam
□きんちょうする
to be nervous
□特に(とくに) especially
□自信(じしん) confidence
□慣れます《なれる》
to get used to

Every year when spring comes, the cherry blossoms bloom.

dictionary form + と

毎年春に　| なると |　桜が咲きます。

例 Ex.
1. このスイッチを押すと、電気がつきます。
2. 朝起きると、頭痛がする。
3. あの店に行くと、いつもあの人に会う。
4. この音楽を聞くと、彼を思い出す。

頭痛	*headache*
思い出す	*to remind*

Point!

- Dictionary form always comes before と.
- A と B: B always happens after A happens. (Ex. 1, 2, and 3)
- と is often used in literature to describe a single event that occurred in the past.
- A useful pattern uses a sense（見る / 聞く）for A and an emotion（思い出す / 泣きたくなる / うれしくなる）for B. This shows that the emotion is always felt when that thing is sensed. (Ex. 4)
- Use なる (become) with i-adjectives : それを見るとうれしくなる。

Dialogue　若い女性二人が話している。

かな： ねえねえ、あそこのケーキ屋さんよって行かない？

みき： え、今レストランで食べたばっかりだよ。

かな： んーわかってるけど、みると食べたくなるんだよね。

みき： ここに来るといつもそうだね。甘い物食べると太るよ。

かな： わかってるけど～。

Common expressions

～といい　*it will be good if*

病気がよくなるといいね。

It will be good if your illness heals.　➡　I hope you get well soon.

The noun 希望（きぼう）also means *hope*, so many students try to say things like 病気がよくなるを希望します. However, you shouldn't use 希望 for casually talking about your personal hopes—use ～といい instead. This expression is often preceded by potential verbs.

明日、晴れるといい

富士山が見られるといい

面接に受かるといい

ないといけない・ないとだめ　*have to*

As with えば, this grammar structure is used for things you need to do.

> はやく起きないといけない。

> ちゃんと食べないとだめだよ。

Watch out!

This usage of と is very similar to えば, so it is sometimes interchangeable.

But えば expresses the speaker's belief, whereas と is based on experiencing the same thing happening previously.

このスイッチを押すと（押せば）、電気がつきます。

朝起きると、頭痛がする ➡ I have a headache when I wake up. (every morning)

朝起きれば、頭痛がする ➡ When I wake up, I will have a headache. → this sounds strange

---

Translation　Two young women are talking.

Kana: Hey, wanna stop by that cake shop?

Miki: Huh? We just ate at the restaurant.

Kana: Yeah I know, but every time I see it I get hungry.

Miki: You're like that whenever we come here. You'll gain weight if you eat sweets.

Kana: I know, but...

新しい言葉　New Words

☐ ケーキ屋さん　cake shop

☐ よって行く　stop by

☐ 甘い物　sweets

Lesson 6 — If spring, I recommend viewing the cherry blossoms.

Topic

春 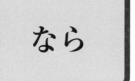 お花見がいいですよ。

> お花見
>   *cherry-blossom viewing*
> 紅葉   *autumn leaves*
> 日光   *Nikko (a city)*
> サーモン   *salmon*

例 Ex.
1. 紅葉が見たいなら日光がおすすめです。
2. 大阪なら、たこ焼きが有名ですよ。
3. あなたが行くなら、私も行きます。
4. おすしは苦手ですけど、サーモンなら食べられます。

Point!

- Verb plain form, a noun or adjective comes before なら.
- なら is mostly used for making recommendations. (Ex. 1, 2)
- A なら B: B is your recommendation.
- This is also used in relation to specific conditions (Ex. 3) and limited conditions. (Ex. 4)

Dialogue ジョーンは会社で同僚と話している。

ジョーン：すみません、ちょっと聞いてもいいですか。
　　　　　着物を買いたいんですが、どこがいいですか？

同僚 A：買い物なら銀座がいいですよ。

同僚 B：銀座はたかいですよ。新宿なら手ごろな着物がありますよ。

ジョーン：そうですか。新宿のどこに行けばいいですか？

同僚 B：私、日曜日なら時間があるから、いっしょに行きましょうか？

ジョーン：わあ、それはたすかります！

Common expressions

(advice)

If ~, then you should / can you~

頭が痛いの？
Your head hurts?
それなら、薬を飲んだほうがいいよ。
If so, you'd better take some medicine.

(condition)

買い物に行くの？
Are you going shopping?
行くなら牛乳買ってきて。
If you go, buy some milk.

火曜日ならいいけど、他の日はだめです。
If it's Tuesday then it's fine, but other days won't work.

Watch out!

Since B is the speaker's opinion or desire, it can't be an inanimate object.

押すなら、ドアが開く ➡ ✗

➡ 押せば、押すと、押したら

Translation　Joan is speaking with her co-workers.

Joan: Excuse me, can I ask you something? I'd like to buy a kimono. Where is a good place for that?

ColleagueA: If you're going shopping, Ginza is good.

ColleagueB: Ginza is expensive. If you go to Shinjuku, you can find reasonable kimonos.

Joan: Oh? Where in Shinjuku should I go?

ColleagueB: If you go on Sunday, I'm free. Shall we go together?

Joan: Wow, that would be a huge help!

新しい言葉　New Words

☐ 手ごろ（てごろ）　reasonable

☐ たすかる　to help (intransitive)

Chapter

1

Lesson 7 — When I go to Japan, I want to see the cherry blossoms.

ta-form + ら

にほんに 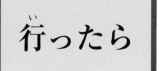 お花見がしたい。

行ったら

例 Ex.

1. このスイッチを押したら、電気がつきます。

2. この資料を読んだら、わかりますよ。

3. 結婚したら、子供が３人欲しい。

4. もし宝くじがあたったら、旅行がしたい。

資料	*document*
もし	*if*
宝くじ	*lottery*

Point!

- たら consists of た form plus ら. Since ta-form indicates past tense, the nuance of たら is usually *after*.

- However, it can also mean *if* or *when* depending on the context. (Ex. 1, 2, and 3)

- もし can be added to the beginning of a sentence to make it clear that *if* is the intended meaning.

Dialogue　青木が上司に話しかけている。

青木：しゅっちょうで韓国に行くんですよね。

上司：うん、そうだよ。

青木：韓国に行ったら、このフェイスマスクを買ってきてくれませんか？（雑誌をみせる）

上司：どこに行ったら買えるの？

青木：このデパートに行ったら買えるみたいです。

上司：そうだなあ。もしそのへんに行ったら買うけど、期待しないで。

青木：お願いします！　（おじぎする）

What's the difference?　たら vs. とき

When used with ta-form, とき refers to a specific point in time rather than a time period.

> 日本_{にっぽん}に着_ついたら、電話_{でんわ}します。
> *After I arrive in Japan, I'll call you.*
> ➡ sometime after arriving

> 日本_{にっぽん}に着_ついたとき、電話_{でんわ}します。
> *When I arrive in Japan, I'll call you.*
> ➡ the exact time or day when you arrive

Although each has a different nuance, you can often use either たら or とき to get your point across. For sentences like the ones below, however, たら is normally used due to the context (they don't reference a specific point in time).

アメリカに帰_{かえ}ったら、大学_{だいがく}に行_いきます。

When (after) I return to US, I will go to the college.

おとなになったら、サッカー選手_{せんしゅ}になりたい。

When I grow up, I want to be a soccer player.

学校_{がっこう}を卒業_{そつぎょう}したら、仕事_{しごと}をさがします。

After I graduate, I'll look for a job.

Translation　Aoki is speaking with her boss.

Aoki: You are going on a business trip to Korea, right?

Boss: Yep.

Aoki: When you go to Korea, could you buy this face mask for me? <shows a magazine>

Boss: Where can I buy it?

Aoki: It looks like you can buy it if you go to this department store.

Boss: Alright, if I go to that area I'll buy it. But don't get your hopes up.

Aoki: I appreciate it! <bows>

新しい言葉　New Words

- □ しゅっちょう　business trip
- □ 期待（きたい）　hope; expectation
- □ そのへん　around there

Imperative and Prohibitive Forms
めいれい形・きんし形

These imperative form and prohibitive forms are used to give commands.

めいれい形活用　Imperative form conjugation

Group 1　Change the final "u" to "e" (except with つ, which becomes て).
　　　　This is the same as the stem for potential form.
Group2　The final る becomes ろ.
Group3　These have irregular conjugations.

Group 1　Change the final "u" to "e".

	辞書形 dictionary form	めいれい形 imperative form
say	言う	言え
hit	打つ	打て
take or get	取る	取れ
die	死ぬ	死ね
call	呼ぶ	呼べ
steal	盗む	盗め
release	放す	放せ
hurry	急ぐ	急げ

* call someone (not used for telephone calls)

Group2　The final る becomes ろ.

raise or lift	あげる	あげろ
lower or get down	さげる	さげろ
stop an action	やめる	やめろ

Group3　These have irregular conjugations.

do	する	しろ
come	来る	来い

"くる"は
むずかしいなぁ

きんし形活用　Prohibitive form conjugation

All groups conjugate the same way: simply add な to the end of dictionary form.

Group 1

	辞書形 dictionary form	きんし形 prohibitive form
use	使う	使うな
stand	立つ	立つな
touch	触る	触るな
die	死ぬ	死ぬな
play	遊ぶ	遊ぶな
walk	歩く	歩くな
swim	泳ぐ	泳ぐな
talk	話す	話すな

Group2

open	開ける	開けるな
close	閉める	閉めるな
turn on	つける	つけるな
turn off	消す	消すな

Group3

do	する	するな
come	来る	来るな

Other command forms

masu-stem ＋ なさい

This command form is used by parents talking to children and teachers talking to students.

Simply attach なさい to the masu-stem of a Group 1, 2, or 3 verb.

Lesson 8 | Come here!

imperative form

こっちに 　来い！

例 Ex.
1. 自分でやれ。
2. はっきり言えよ。
3. これを見ろ。
4. さっさと仕事しろ。

やれ《やる》 *do*
はっきり *clearly*
さっさと *quickly*

Point!

● This imperative form is typically used by men when speaking to their children or subordinates.

● It sounds very rough, so women usually use te-form without ください instead（来て, 見て, 言って, etc.) or 〜なさい. (see page 33)

● It is often used with adverbs like はっきり and さっさと. (Ex. 2, 3)

Dialogue　野球部の監督と部員

監督：みんな集まれ！
部員：はい！
監督：遅いぞ、はやくしろ！
　　　（みんな集まる）
監督：これが最後の試合だ。
　　　おもいきっていけ！
部員：はい！

Common expressions

One more thing...

Imperative form can be used with causative form （せる or させる）, in which case the final る becomes ろ. This is used for giving commands and making requests.

私<small>わたし</small>にやらせろ

let me do it

彼<small>かれ</small>にやらせろ

let him / make him do it

If the subject of a causative verb is the speaker, the meaning will be *let me* rather than the "force" nuance. But with other subjects, the meaning will depend on the context (see page 46).

Translation	A baseball-team coach and players.
Coach:	Everyone, come over here!
Members:	Yes, coach!
Coach:	Too slow! Hurry up!
	This is the last game.
	Give it your all! Go!
Members:	Ok!

新しい言葉　New Words

□監督（かんとく）　coach

□集まれ《あつまる》　to gather

□部員（ぶいん）　member of a club

□はやく　quickly

□最後（さいご）　final; last

□おもいきって《おもいきる》
　　　　　　　　give it your all

Don't tell anyone.

prohibitive form

だれ
誰にも

はな
話すな。

例 Ex.

1. 危（あぶ）ないから、行（い）くな！

2. さわるな！

3. あきらめるなよ。

4. そう言（い）うなって。

> 負けるな《まける》 *to lose*
> 危ない *dangerous*

Point!

- Imperative form is mostly used by men to give commands. Women use ないで instead, which is the negative te-form without ください.

- 行（い）かないで　あきらめないで　おくれないで

- This form is sometimes used to encourage someone, in which case endings like よ and って are often added. (Ex. 3, 4) The ending って comes from 〜と（って）いっている meaning *I'm saying〜*.

Dialogue　居酒屋で男二人が話している。

青木：最近、ツイてないよ。

織田：なにがあったの？

青木：彼女とケンカしたり……

織田：ケンカなんてよくあるよ。気にするな。

青木：それに、会社のめんせつも落ちたしさ。ダメだな〜。

織田：よわきになるなって。

青木：お前はいいよな。いい会社に就職できたし、彼女はやさしいしさ。

織田：そう言うなって。おいおい、飲みすぎるなよ。

Common expressions with imperative form and prohibitive form

Hand over the money!!
かねをだせ!!

Get your hands up!!
手をあげろ!!

Don't move!!
うごくな!!

Don't dilly-dally!!
ぐずぐずするな!!

Hurry up!!
いそげ!!

Stop!!
まて!!
Get out of here!
にげろ!

Translation Two guys are talking at a Japanese bar.

Aoki: I've had a run of bad luck lately.

Oda: What happened?

Aoki: I fought with my girlfriend...

Oda: Fighting like that isn't rare. Don't worry about it.

Aoki: Also, I failed my job interview. I'm worthless.

Oda: Don't be negative.

Aoki: You've got it good. You got a job at a good company and your girlfriend is kind.

Oda: Don't say it like that. Hey, don't drink too much!

新しい言葉 New Words

- □ ツイてない　bad luck
- □ ケンカ　fight; argument
- □ よくある　happens a lot
- □ 気にする　worry about
- □ めんせつ　interview
- □ よわき　negative feelings
- □ 就職 (しゅうしょく)　get a job

imperative/prohibitive form

止_とまれ と書_かいてあります。

ドア　*door*
さわるな《さわる》　*touch*
知らない人　*stranger*
はやく　*quickly*

例 Ex.
1. ドアに入_{はい}るなと書_かいてありますよ。

2. これは、さわるなっていう意味_{いみ}です。

3. 母_{はは}は知_しらない人_{ひと}に気_きをつけろと言_いいました。

4. はやくしろって言_いったのに。

⌐Point!⌐

● When describing information written on something like a sign or piece of paper, use と書_かいてあります. (Ex. 1)

● ～てあります is used for describing the state of something.

● という意味_{いみ}です is used to explain the meaning of a word or phrase. (Ex. 2)

● Ex. 4 is a sort of confirmation: "I told you..."

Dialogue　マイクが壁に貼ってあるお知らせについて、となりの人に聞いている。

マイク：すみません、これなんて書いてあります
　　　　か？
　　　　漢字が難しくて読めません。

となり：朝8時までにごみを出せって書いてありま
　　　　す。
　　　　それから、指定の袋を使えって書いてあり
　　　　ますね。

マイク：指定の袋ってどんな袋ですか。どこで買え
　　　　ますか？

となり：スーパーで買えますよ。
　　　　ちょっと待ってください。今持ってきて
　　　　みせますよ。

Signs

Prohibited Actions

さわるな
don't touch

走_{はし}るな
don't run

ペット入_{はい}るな
pets not allowed

ごみ捨_すてるな
don't litter

Other Signs

止_とまれ
stop

温泉_{おんせん}
onsen

郵便局_{ゆうびんきょく}
post office

初心者_{しょしんしゃ}
beginner (newly-licensed driver)

Store Signs

open

closed (for preparing)

closed (for holiday)

Waste

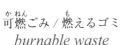
可燃_{かねん}ごみ / 燃_もえるゴミ
burnable waste

不燃_{ふねん}ごみ / 燃_もえないゴミ
unburnable waste

粗大_{そだい}ゴミ / 大型_{おおがた}ごみ
oversized waste

Translation Mike is asking his next-door neighbor about a notice on the wall.

Mike: Excuse me, what does it says here? The kanji are difficult so I can't read it.

Neighbor: It says take out the garbage by eight in the morning. And use the designated bag.

Mike: What sort of bag is designated? Where can I buy it?

Neighbor: You can buy them at the supermarket. Just a moment. I'll bring one and show you.

新しい言葉 New Words
- □ ごみ garbage
- □ 指定(してい) designated
- □ 袋(ふくろ) bag

Passive Form 受身形

Unlike the passive form in English, the Japanese passive form has various usages.

1. The speaker is bothered by something

2. The sentence doesn't have a subject

3. It's a historical topic

4. Formal speech

As you can see, each of these has a different nuance, so they can sometimes be confusing. However, with practice you will learn which meaning is intended from the overall context.

- Some verbs don't have a passive form, like 違う (*chigau*).
- The 尊敬語 (*sonkeigo*) form of a verb is identical to its passive form. So by learning these conjugations, you are also getting a major head start on the daunting task of understanding Japanese honorific language.

Sentence structure

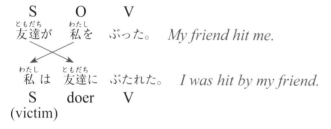

$$\begin{array}{ccc} S & O & V \\ 友達が & 私を & ぶった。 \end{array}$$ *My friend hit me.*

私は 友達に ぶたれた。 *I was hit by my friend.*
S doer V
(victim)

If the sentence has a direct object, don't make it the subject.

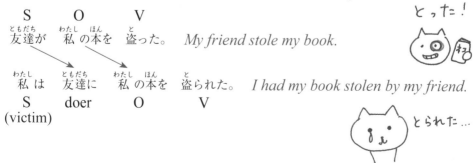

S O V
友達が 私の本を 盗った。 *My friend stole my book.*

とった！

私は 友達に 私の本を 盗られた。 *I had my book stolen by my friend.*
S doer O V
(victim)

とられた...

受身形活用 Passive form conjugation

Group 1　Use the nai-form of a verb to create its passive form—simply replace ない with れる.

	ない形 nai-form	受身形 passive form
invite	誘わない	誘われる
hit	ぶたない	ぶたれる
steal	盗らない	盗られる
die	死なない	死なれる
call	呼ばない	呼ばれる
step	踏まない	踏まれる
cry	泣かない	泣かれる
hurry	急がない	急がれる
wake	起こさない	起こされる

Group2　The final る becomes られる.

bully	いじめる	いじめられる
praise	ほめる	ほめられる
quit	辞める	辞められる

Group3　These verbs have irregular conjugations.

do	しない	される
come	来ない	来られる

Lesson 11 | I was dumped by my girlfriend.

Victim は / が　　　doer に　　　passive verb

僕(ぼく)は　　　彼女(かのじょ)に　　　**ふられ**　　　ました。

例(Ex.)
1. 友達(ともだち)は先生(せんせい)に叱(しか)られました。
2. 蚊(か)に刺(さ)された。
3. 犬(いぬ)に手(て)をかまれた。
4. 頭(あたま)を叩(たた)かれた。

> ふられた《ふる》 *to be damped*
> 叱られた《しかる》 *to be scolded*
> 蚊 *mosquito*
> 刺された《さす》 *to be bit (by a bug)*
> かまれた《かむ》 *to be bit (by an animal)*

Point!

- This passive form is used when the action of the verb is undesirable, which is why it is sometimes referred to as the "troubled passive." The subject of the sentence is the one in trouble.

- Victim は（　）passive form of verb　　私(わたし)は（　）さされた
  The doer of the action is marked with に:　　蚊(か)に
  If stating a direct object, like a body part:　　手(て)を
  私(わたし)は　蚊(か)に　手(て)を　刺(さ)された　Depending on the focus, stating the entire sentence might not be necessary.

- Be careful which particle you use:
  蚊(か)に刺(さ)された　the focus is 蚊(か)　(Ex.2)
  手(て)を刺(さ)された　the focus is 手(て)　(Ex.4)
  私(わたし)が刺(さ)された the focus is 私(わたし)

ちょっと―

Dialogue　朝の職場でマイクと青木が話している。

マイク：朝の電車は混んでるから、毎日押されたり、足をふまれた
　　　　りして本当にいやですね。

青　木：ぼくは、ちかんとまちがえられましたよ。

マイク：えええ。

青　木：ぼくの手がちょうど女の人のおしりにあたって……。

マイク：そうか……。女の人はおしりをさわられたと思ったんです
　　　　ね。

Common expressions using troubled passive

財布を盗まれた
wallet was stolen

顔を殴られた
face was punched

クラスメイトにいじめられた
was bullied by a classmate

銃で撃たれた
was shot with a gun

車にひかれた
was run over

誰かに殺された
was killed by someone

* By making the victim the subject, the troubled passive form focuses on his or her feelings. This is in contrast to English, which tends to make the antagonist or criminal the subject. It's a subtle distinction, but one that reveals something about the Japanese mindset and culture.

Watch out!

These are exceptions to the negative nuance of troubled passive; they indicate pleasant feelings or situations.

僕は先生にほめられた。　*I was praised by my teacher.*

私は大切な仕事を上司に任された。　*My boss entrusted me an important job.*

友達にパーティーに誘われた。　*I was invited a party by my friend.*

Translation Mike and Aoki are talking at their office in the morning.

Mike: I really hate the train in the morning. It's so crowded that every day I get pushed around and my feet stepped on.

Aoki: I was mistaken for a groper.

Mike: What?!

Aoki: My hand just happened to hit a woman's butt.

Mike: I see. She thought you intentionally touched her butt.

新しい言葉　New Words

☐ 押されたり　to be pushed
☐ ふまれたり　to be stepped on
☐ ちかん　groper
☐ おしり　butt

Lesson 12　English is spoken all over the world.

S は / が　　　　place/material で　　　　passive verb

英語は　　世界中で　　話され　　ています。

例 Ex.
1. オリンピックが東京で開かれます。
2. このパソコンは中国で作られました。
3. このパンはお米で作られている。
4. 「老人と海」はヘミングウェイによって書かれた。

> オリンピック　The Olympics
> 開かれる《ひらく》　to hold an event
> ヘミングウェイ　Hemingway
> 老人と海　The Old Man and the Sea

Point!

● This passive form can be used to express the idiomatic English meaning of *They say that...* or *It is said that...*

● It is used with 〜ている, which shows a continuous state ➡ されている

● It is also used for official announcement. (Ex. 1)

● This passive form can also mean *made in* or *made of.* (Ex. 2, 3)

● Use によって when you want to clearly specify the person or organization that did an action. This is particularly used for historical events. (Ex. 4)

Dialogue　ツアーガイドがお寺の説明をしている。

ガイド：このお寺は743年に、建てられました。
　　　　1998年には、世界いさんに登録されました。
　　　　また、こちらの大仏は「奈良の大仏」として知られています。
観光客：誰が作ったんですか？
ガイド：聖武天皇によって作られました。
観光客：そうですか〜。

Common expressions

多くの人に読まれている
read by many people

昔から言われている
has been said since ancient times

5か国語に翻訳された
translated into five languages

シュリーマンによって遺跡が発見された
ruins were discovered by Schliemann

電話はベルによって発明された
the telephone was invented by Bell

Watch out!

The passive sentence pattern 「～によって—された」 sounds very formal, so active sentences are used instead for informal conversation.

シュリーマンによって遺跡が発見された ➡ シュリーマンが遺跡を発見した。

If you don't specify the doer of the action, however, you can use the passive form even in informal speech.

遺跡が発見された。

Translation A tour guide is describing a temple.

Guide: This temple was built in 743. In 1998, it was registered as a World Heritage Site. Also, this giant Buddha statue is known as *nara no daibutsu*.

Tourist: Who made it?

Guide: It was created by Emperor Shōmu.

Tourist: I see.

新しい言葉 New Words

□ 建てられた《たてる》 was built

□ 世界いさん World Heritage Site

□ 登録(とうろく) registration

□ 大仏(だいぶつ) giant Buddha statue

□ 聖武天皇 Emperor Shōmu

Causative Form 使役形(しえきけい)

Causative form has two usages depending the context.

1. Forcing

    母(はは)は私(わたし)に野菜(やさい)を食(た)べさせる。   *My mom forces me to eat vegetables.*

2. Permission

    母(はは)は私(わたし)にお菓子(かし)を食(た)べさせる。   *My mom lets me eat snacks.*

Sentence structure

S	O	V
母(はは)は	私(わたし)に	野菜(やさい)を	食(た)べさせる

S	O	V
母(はは)は	私(わたし)を	急(いそ)がせる

The conjugation is similar to passive form.

Group1   For Group 1 verbs, the passive form ending れる becomes せる.

	受身形(うけみけい) passive form	使役形(しえきけい) causative form
meet	会(あ)われる	会(あ)わせる
wait	待(ま)たれる	待(ま)たせる
steal	盗(と)られる	盗(と)らせる
drink	飲(の)まれる	飲(の)ませる
hurry	急(いそ)がれる	急(いそ)がせる

Group 2   For Group 2 verbs, られる becomes させる.

eat	食(た)べられる	食(た)べさせる
open	開(あ)けられる	開(あ)けさせる

Group 3   Irregular

do	される	させる
come	来(こ)られる	来(こ)させる

Causative-passive form 使役受身

Just as with passive form, the subject of a causative-passive verb is the person who does the action.

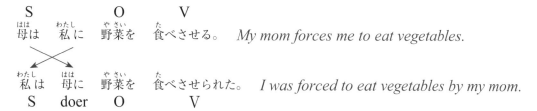

To create the causative-passive form, simply change the causative ending させる to させられる. However, the abbreviated form される is typically used for Group 1 verbs, with one notable exception: Group 1 verbs whose dictionary form ends in す change to させられる to avoid the use of double さ（さされる）, which is difficult to pronounce.

Group 1　Just put さ before れる of passive form. れる → される

	使役形 causative form	使役受身形 causative-passive form
wait	待たせる	待たされる
make	作らせる	作らされる
go	行かせる	行かされる
smoke	吸わせる	吸わされる
speak or talk	話させる	話させられる

Group 2　Use させられる as described above.

eat	食べさせる	食べさせられる
give up	あきらめさせる	あきらめさせられる
open	開けさせる	開けさせられる
close	閉めさせる	閉めさせられる

Group 3　Irregular

do	させる	させられる
come	来させる	来させられる

Lesson 13　The mother makes her child eat vegetables.

doer　は/が　person　に　　　　　　　　　　causative verb

母親（ははおや）　は　子供（こども）　に　野菜（やさい）を　食べ（た）させる。

例 Ex.
1. 部長（ぶちょう）は部下（ぶか）に残業（ざんぎょう）させた。
2. 先生（せんせい）は生徒（せいと）に漢字（かんじ）をたくさん書（か）かせた。
3. 先輩（せんぱい）が（私（わたし）に）重（おも）い荷物（にもつ）を持（も）たせた。
4. 笑（わら）わせないで。

部長	*manager*
部下	*subordinate*
残業	*overtime work*
先輩	*senior worker or student*
笑わせないで《笑う》	
	don't make me laugh

Point!

- This is used when someone is forced to do something. (Ex. 1)
- When a direct object is specified it is marked with を; the particle に is attached to the person being forced (the indirect object).
- This also can be used for negative statements. (Ex. 4)
- It can be used to create the pattern *Don't make <verb>*. (Ex. 4)

Dialogue　小学校の先生が生徒の親と話している。

先生：お子さんはお家ではどんなようすですか。

母親：そうですね……。うちに帰ったら、まず宿題をさせています。
　　　それと、週に２回は、スイミングと英会話に行かせています。
　　　週末は空手も習わせているんです。それから、そろばんも。

先生：忙しいですね。あまり無理させないほうがいいと思いますよ。

Common expressions

お待たせしました。
Sorry for the wait.

30分も!!

待たせてすみません。
I'm very sorry for the wait.

お待たせしました is very commonly heard in restaurants and stores.

お <verb stem> しました is a formal structure known as *kenjōgo* (see page 62).

If it was a long wait, お待たせしてすみません is used.

心配させてごめん。
Sorry for making you worry.

心配させないで。
Don't make me worry.

がっかりさせてごめん。
Sorry for making you disappointed.

What's the difference? 生徒 vs. 学生、母 vs. お母さん vs. 母親

With 生徒, the viewpoint is that of the teacher or mentor, so the nuance is similar to pupil. But if you are the student and referring to yourself or another student, use 学生 (this describes your "profession" or "occupation").

母 is used by adults when referring to their own mothers. お母さん is similar to *mom* in English, but it is not always the speaker's own mom—it can be anyone's mom. The formal way to refer to someone else's mother is 母親.

Translation An elementary-school teacher is speaking with the parent of a student.

Teacher: How is your child at home?

Mother: Well, I make him do his homework first when he gets home.

I also make him go swimming class and English lessons twice a week. And on the weekends, he goes karate and abacus lessons too.

Teacher: Wow, he is busy. I think you shouldn't push him so hard.

新しい言葉 New Words

- □ようす　state, condition
- □宿題(しゅくだい)　homework
- □スイミング　swimming
- □英会話　English-conversation class
- □無理させる (むり)　force someone to do the impossible
- □そろばん　abacus

Lesson 14 — The mother let her child eat his favorite thing.

doer	は／が	person	に	object	causative verb

母親（ははおや）は　子供（こども）に　好（す）きなものを　食（た）べさせる。

例 Ex.

1. 鈴木先生（すずきせんせい）は、私（わたし）たちに自由（じゆう）に研究（けんきゅう）をさせてくれる。

2. 犬（いぬ）を広（ひろ）い公園（こうえん）で遊（あそ）ばせてあげる。

3. 子供（こども）の時（とき）、両親（りょうしん）はバレエを習（なら）わせてくれた。

4. 具合（ぐあい）が悪（わる）いので、今日（きょう）は休（やす）ませてください。

自由に	*freely*
研究する	*to research*
バレエ	*ballet*
具合	*condition*
具合が悪い	*to feel sick (idiom)*

Point!

- This usage of causative form shows permission and is equivalent to the English *let*. (Ex. 1)
- It is often used together with 〜てあげる or 〜てくれる to further indicate the meaning of *let*. (Ex. 1, 2, and 3)
- You can use this for making requests (*Please let me…*). (Ex. 4)

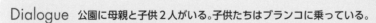

Dialogue　公園に母親と子供2人がいる。子供たちはブランコに乗っている。

上の子：ねえねえ。私の番だよ。やらせて。

下の子：ちょっと待って〜。

母：みか、やらせてあげなさい！

男：かわいいですね。写真を一枚とらせてください。

母：えっ、いいですけど、はずかしいわ〜

男：いや、あの……お子さんの写真です……。

50

Watch out!

These phrases are common in English, but Japanese people usually don't use causative here.

チェックさせて ➡ チェックする
let me check ➡ *I'll check*

みさせて ➡ みせて
let me see ➡ *show me*

いかせます ➡ じゃ、そろそろ…。
let you go ➡ *Well, it's about time...*
(you should be going)

Literally, let you go is いかせます. But it sounds very arrogant in Japanese, そろそろ means it is about time to ~ and sounds consider the other person.

One more thing

Increasing levels of politeness with causative

休^{やす}ませて

休^{やす}ませてくれる

休^{やす}ませてください

休^{やす}ませてもらえますか ➡ potential form of もらう

休^{やす}ませていただけますか ➡ honorific form of もらう

休^{やす}ませていただけませんか ➡ The negative form is most polite.

Translation A mother and her two kids are at park.
The kids are on swing.

Older child: Hey, it's my turn. Let me do it.

Younger child: Not yet...

Mother: Mika, let her do it!

Man: So cute! Please allow me to take a picture.

Mother: Oh, sure, but I'm shy you know...

Man: I mean a picture of your kids...

新しい言葉 New Words

☐ ねえねえ hey

☐ 私の番(ばん) my turn

☐ ブランコ swing

The child was forced to eat the vegetables by his mom.

S	は / が	doer		object		causative verb

子供 は 母親 に 野菜 を 食べさせられた。

例 Ex.

1. 部下は部長に残業させられた。

2. 友達にジュースをおごらされた。

3. 彼に待たされた。

4. 休みなのに会社に来させられた。

おごらされた《おごる》
to be forced to treat

Point!

- The sentence structure is the same as passive form (the doer of the action is marked with に, while the person affected is the subject).
- Group 2, 3 verbs end in させられた. (Ex. 1, 4)
- Group 1 verbs end in された. (Ex. 2, 3)
- When the subject is *I*, it is typically omitted, so the doer of the action will be at the beginning of the sentence. (Ex. 2, 3)

Dialogue　仕事から帰ってきた夫は酔っぱらっている。

夫：ただいま〜

妻：おかえり。おそかったじゃない？

夫：ああ、部長につきあわされてさ……。

妻：たくさん飲んだの？

夫：いや、飲みたくなかったんだけど、飲まされたんだよ。

妻：ふ〜ん。ほんとう？

Common expressions

嫌な仕事をやらされた。
I was forced to do annoying tasks.

無理に言わされた。
I was forced to say something (that I didn't want to).

父に手伝わされた。
I was forced to help my father.

10周も走らされた。
I was forced to run 10 laps.

高い物を買わされた。
I was forced to buy something expensive.

買い物に行かされた。
I was forced to go shopping.

Watch out !

させられる is hard to say even for native speakers, so in conversation they will often say phrases like the ones below instead.

母にマンガを捨てさせられた ➡ 母がマンガを捨てろって言った。

父に早く寝させられた ➡ 父に早く寝ろって言われた。

先生に遅刻の理由を話させられた ➡ 先生が遅刻の理由を話せって。

Translation **A husband returned home from work drunk.**

Husband: I'm home~

Wife: Oh, you're quite late aren't you?

Husband: Yeah, my boss made me go drinking with him.

Wife: Did you drink a lot?

Husband: I didn't want to, but he forced me to drink.

Wife: Hmm. Is that so?

新しい言葉 New Words

□つきあわされてさ《つきあう》
　　　　　go with someone

□ふ〜ん　a sound of annoyance or disbelief

Keigo 敬語(けいご)

です and ます style of speech is called *teineigo* (*teinei* means polite), however, there is a type of speech that is more polite. This style is known as 敬語(けいご) (*keigo*). There are two types of *keigo*: *sonkeigo* (respect) and *kenjōgo* (humble). It is commonly referred to as "honorific" in Japanese language instruction.

Sonkeigo subject = the other party (a boss, customer, elderly person, teacher, etc.)

Kenjōgo subject = you or people close to you

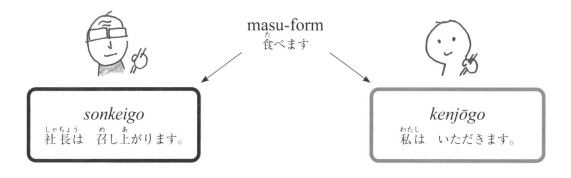

Special verbs

sonkeigo	*teineigo* (masu-form)	*kenjōgo*
召(め)し上(あ)がります	食(た)べます　飲(の)みます	いただきます
おっしゃいます	言(い)います	申(もう)します
いらっしゃいます	行(い)きます　来(き)ます	参(まい)ります
いらっしゃいます	います	おります
ご覧(らん)になります	見(み)ます	拝見(はいけん)します
ご存知(ぞんじ)です	知(し)ります	存(ぞん)じております
なさいます	します	いたします
くださいます	くれます	
お受(う)け取(と)りになります	もらいます	いただきます
いらっしゃいます	訪(たず)ねます	伺(うかが)います
おかけになります	座(すわ)ります	座(すわ)らせていただきます

Other verbs

sonkeigo お(masu-stem)になります	*teineigo*	*kenjōgo* お(masu-stem)します
お書きになります	書きます	お書きします
お話しになります	話します	お話しします
お読みになります	読みます	お読みします

The above *keigo* phrases appear similar, but they have different endings. These endings will clue you in as to the subject of the sentence.

Present progressive: be ~ing ています

sonkeigo ていらっしゃいます	*teineigo*	*kenjōgo* ております
住んでいらっしゃいます	住んでいます	住んでおります

Respectfully giving advice

お (*sonkeigo*　noun or te-form) ください

noun

召し上がります　　　➡　お召し上がりください。

ご覧になります　　　➡　ご覧ください。

お受け取りになります ➡　お受け取りください。

おかけになります　　➡　おかけください。

te-form

いらっしゃいます　　➡　いらっしゃってください。

おっしゃいます　　　➡　おっしゃってください。

Passive: Sometimes passive form is used for *sonkeigo*.

社長は帰りました　　➡　社長は帰られました。

The company president will have a beer.

S   sonkeigo

社長 が ビール を 召し上がります。

例 Ex.　These verbs are special, and some have several meanings. (see page 54)

1. お客様は３時にいらっしゃいます。

2. 資料をご覧になりましたか。

3. 先生、今なんとおっしゃいましたか。

4. 先生がおみやげをくださいました。

> 資料　*document*
> なんと　なに＋と　*what*
> おみやげ　*souvenir*

Point!

- These are very polite expressions known as "honorifics."
- They show the speaker's respect toward the other party.
- The subject is a person who is older than you or in a higher social position.

Dialogue　はるかが義理の母のかずこと話している。

はるか：お母様、なにか召し上がりますか？

かずこ：ああ、ありがとう。じゃ、お茶をもらおうかしら。

はるか：東京にいらっしゃったのは、ひさしぶりですね。

かずこ：そうねえ。５年ぶりね。

はるか：そうですか。もうスカイツリーはごらんになりましたか。

かずこ：まだなのよ。行きたかったけど。

はるか：今日はおつかれでしょうから、どうぞごゆっくりなさってください。

Special verbs that show respect

召<ruby>め</ruby>し上<ruby>あ</ruby>がる
eat or drink

おっしゃる
speak

いらっしゃる
come or go

ごらんになる
see or view

ご存知<ruby>ぞんじ</ruby>だ
know

なさる
do

くださる
give

お受<ruby>う</ruby>け取<ruby>と</ruby>りになる
receive

かける
sit

お休<ruby>やす</ruby>みになる
sleep or rest

Watch out !

The plain form of some of these verbs ends in る, so you'd think their masu-form would end in ります —but it actually ends in います.

おっしゃいます　　いらっしゃいます　　なさいます　　くださいます

Within a sentence, honorific verbs will have a form and tense that matches the context, just like any other verb.

おっしゃった時<ruby>とき</ruby>
when you said

いらっしゃる前<ruby>まえ</ruby>
before you come

なさるので
because you do

Translation Haruka is talking to Kazuko, her mother-in-law.

Haruko: Would you like something to drink?

Kazuko: Oh, thank you. Well then, could I have a cup of tea?

Haruka: It's been a long time since you came to Tokyo.

Kazuko: Yes. It's been five years.

Haruka: Oh, I see. Did you see the Skytree yet?

Kazuko: Not yet. But I wanted to go to it.

Haruka: I imagine you are tired today, so please rest.

新しい言葉　New Words

□ 義理の母　mother-in-law

□ お母様（おかあさま）
respectful way to address a mother

□ かしら　I guess or I wonder (feminine)

The company president will read the book.

S　　　は / が　　　　　　　　　　　　　　　　sonkeigo

| 社長（しゃちょう） | は | 本（ほん）を | お読（よ）みになります。 |

例 Ex.

1. お箸（はし）はお使（つか）いになりますか？
2. これから教授（きょうじゅ）がお話（はな）しになります。
3. 袋（ふくろ）はご利用（りよう）になりますか？
4. 少々（しょうしょう）お待（ま）ちください。

教授	*professor*
利用	*to use*
少々	*a little (formal)*

Point!

● Verbs that don't have a special form to show respect use the following pattern:

　　お + masu-stem + になります　(Ex. 1 and 2)
　　　　　　　or
　　ご + masu-stem + になります　(Ex. 3)

　　As a general rule, ご is the prefix used with words consisting of two kanji, but there are exceptions (see page 68).

● Sonkeigo + ください is used to respectfully give advice. (Ex. 4)

Dialogue　ホテルの受付で

青木：すみません、ネットで予約した青木です。

受付：いらっしゃいませ。青木様ですね。本日はありがとうございます。
　　　朝食つき一泊でよろしいですか。

青木：はい。大浴場はありますか？

受付：はい、深夜2時までご利用になれます。

青木：わかりました。

受付：外出の時はこちらにカギをおわたしください。では、ごゆっくり。

Common expressions

お買いになる
buy

お急ぎになる
hurry

お借りになる
borrow

お乗りになる
ride

Watch out !

Since the ます stem acts like a noun, です is used instead of になります. This is especially true with the following verbs.

持つ ➡ ポイントカードは、お持ちですか？ *Do you have a point card?*

住まう ➡ どちらにお住まいですか？ *Where do you live?*

勤める ➡ どちらにお勤めですか？ *Where do you work?*

These can also be used with ください to respectfully give advice.

お持ちください。 *Please take this (for your own benefit).*

And with special verbs too:

お召し上がりください。　ご覧ください。

Note: いらっしゃる and おっしゃる use te-form with ください：
いらっしゃってください。　おっしゃってください。

Translation At a hotel reception desk.

Aoki: Excuse me, I made a reservation online. The name is Aoki.

Receptionist: Welcome, Mr. Aoki. Thank you for choosing to stay with us today. A one-night stay with a breakfast, right?

Aoki: Yes. Is there a public bath here?

Receptionist: Yes, you may use our public bath until two in the morning.

Aoki: Okay.

Receptionist: Please leave your room key here when you go outside. Enjoy your stay!

新しい言葉 New Words

☐つき included　☐一泊 one night

☐深夜 (late) night　☐外出 going out

☐大浴場(だいよくじょう)　public bath

Lesson 18 | I will have a glass of wine.

S は / が　　　　　　　　　　　　　　kenjōgo

私　は　ワインを一杯(いっぱい)、　いただきます。

> These are special verbs, some of which have several meanings. (see p. 54)

例 Ex.
1. イタリアから参(まい)りました。
2. お手紙(てがみ)を拝見(はいけん)しました。
3. 本日(ほんじつ)は、10時(じ)から営業(えいぎょう)しております。
4. 明日(あす)、そちらに伺(うかが)います。

手紙	*letter*
本日	*today (formal)*
営業	*operate; open*

┌ **Point!** ┐
- These are humble expressions called *kenjōgo*.
- The subject is a speaker expressing a humble attitude toward another other party who is older or in a higher social position.
- It is often used in restaurants, stores, and business situations.

Dialogue　記者が画家にインタビューをしている。

クリス：はじめまして。クリスと申します。
　　　　イギリスから参りました。よろしくお願いいたします。
画　家：こちらこそ。日本語がとても上手ですね。
クリス：ありがとうございます。
　　　　ロンドンで先生の展覧会を拝見しました。
　　　　それについてお話を伺いたいんですが。
画　家：はい、いいですよ。

Common expressions

申す *to speak; to say; to be called*

小川と申します。
My name is Ogawa.

先ほど申しましたように…。
As I said a moment ago...

おる *to be*

今日は家におります。
I will be at home today.

ておる

英語を勉強しております。
I am studying English.

いたす *to do*

お手伝いいたします。
I will help you.

お調べいたします。
I will look into it.

存じる *to know*

存じております。
I know (that).

伺う *to ask; to visit; to call upon*

ご注文を伺います。
I will take (ask) your order now.

伺いたいのですが。
I'd like to ask you something.

Watch out !

あります and です become ございます and でございます, respectively. This is often thought of as *kenjōgo*, but it is actually *teineigo*—so the subject doesn't matter. It is just more polite than です and あります.

です ➡ でございます。

place にあります ➡ にございます。

noun があります ➡ がございます。

主語はなんでもいいんだ
The subject can be anything

お手洗いはあちらにございます。 *The bathroom is over there.*
質問がございますか？ *Do you have any questions?*

Translation **A journalist is interviewing an artist.**

Chris: Nice to meet you. My name is Chris. I came here from England. It is nice to meet you.

Artist: Nice to meet you too. Your Japanese is very good.

Chris: Thank you very much. I saw your exhibition in London.

I would like to ask you about that.

Artist: Sure, that's fine.

新しい言葉 New Words

□展覧会(てんらんかい)
exhibition

□記者(きしゃ)
journalist; reporter

S　　は / が　　　　　　　　　　　kenjōgo

私（わたし）　　が　　　　　お手伝（てつだ）いします。

例 Ex.

1. お読（よ）みしましょうか。
2. 改札口（かいさつぐち）でお待（ま）ちしております。
3. 申（もう）し込（こ）み用紙（ようし）をお渡（わた）しします。
4. ご連絡（れんらく）いたします。

改札口	*ticket gate*
申込用紙	*application form*
お渡し《わたす》	*to hand*

Point!

- Verbs that don't have special humble forms follow the patterns below.
  お + masu-stem + します。
  ご + masu-stem + します。
- This is similar to the respectful patterns, the only difference is how you end the sentence. The respectful form ends in になります, whereas the humble form ends in します。
- Sometimes いたします is used instead of します. They have the same meaning, but いたします is more formal.

Dialogue　旅館で

仲居：いらっしゃいませ。お部屋にご案内いたします。
　客：お世話になります。
仲居：お荷物をお持ちします。
　客：すみません。*

――部屋で――

仲居：お食事は6時にご用意いたします。
　　　お食事後にお布団をひきにまいります。
　　　どうぞごゆっくり。

*すみません is often closer to thank you than *I'm sorry*.

Other humble expressions

～ていただきます　　te-form + いただきます　　*I will*

書類を送っていただきました。
I had him send the document.

日本語を教えて
いただけますか / ませんか？
Could you teach me Japanese?

～せていただきます　　causative + ていただきます　　*let me*

お休みさせて
いただいてもよろしいでしょうか。
*Would it be alright if I took
the day off?*

日時を変更させていただきます。
*Please allow me to change
the schedule.*

～てもよろしいでしょうか　　te-form + よろしいでしょうか。　　*May I*

お借りしてもよろしいでしょうか？
Is it okay if I borrow that?

今、お話ししても
よろしいでしょうか？
*Would it be alright to speak
with you?*

Translation　At a ryokan (a Japanese-style inn)

Employee: Welcome! Please allow me to show you
to your room.

Customer: Thank you.

Employee: Shall I take your belongings?

Customer: Oh, Thank you.

—In the room—

Employee: A meal will be served at 6:00, after which
I will return to prepare your bed. Please
relax and enjoy your stay.

新しい言葉　New Words

□仲居　waitress at a ryokan

□お世話になります
lit. *it will be in your care*, this
phrase can imply anything
from a simple thank you to "I'm
looking forward to working
with you."

Lesson 20 The company president returned home.

S　　は / が　　　　　　　　　　sonkeigo (passive form)

| 社長 | は　家　に | 帰られました。 |

辞められる《やめる》 *to quit*
忘年会 *a party at the end of the year*
参加（する）*to participate*
部下 *subordinate*

例 Ex.　1. 先生は、大阪に行かれました。

2. 山田さんは、会社を辞められました。

3. このことについて、どう思われますか？

4. 忘年会に参加されますか？

Point!

● As we have learned, one usage of passive form is to indicate a troublesome action or state.

● So how do you know if it is troubled passive or honorific passive? The context will tell you. Consider these two sentences:

山田さんは、仕事を辞められました。　　山田さんは、部下に会社を辞められました。
Mr. Yamada quit his job.　　　　　　　Mr. Yamada had a subordinate quit on him.

● The sentence on the left is honorific passive, because there is no other possible actor for the verb except Mr. Yamada. But the sentence on the right has an indirect object (部下) marked with に, so we know that Mr. Yamada isn't the one who quit. Therefore, that usage must be troubled passive.

Dialogue 父親と息子が久しぶりに友人に会っている。

細井：お久しぶりです。お子さん、大きくなられましたね。

小川：ああ、もう中学生だよ。サッカー部でがんばってるんだ。

細井：サッカー部ですか。小川さんも一緒にやられるんですか？

小川：うん、時々ね。お、こんな時間だ。帰らないと。

細井：タクシーで帰られますか？

What's the difference? いらっしゃる vs. 行かれる

While both of these verbs mean *to go*, 行かれる is considered less polite than いらっしゃる. This is also true for the お____になります pattern— it is more polite than the passive form equivalent.

使われますか　　　　　お使いになりますか

Since the potential form of a Group 2 verb is identical to its honorific passive form, the latter is typically only used with Group 1 verbs to avoid confusion.

Group 1	Group 2
• potential: 話せます • honorific passive: 話されます	• potential: 食べられます • honorific passive: 食べられます
These are clearly different, so there is no confusion.	These are identical, so honorific passive tends to be avoided.

Watch out！二重敬語 Double Keigo

Some Japanese people use passive form at the end of the respectful pattern, but this is a mistake! It is an incorrect structure created by people trying to be even more polite.

ご覧になられます　incorrect　　　おっしゃられます　incorrect

➡ ご覧になります　correct　　　➡ おっしゃいます correct

おめしあがりになられまして..

はい おひさしぶりいからられ..？

too much

Translation　A father and son are meeting a friend for the first time in a while.

Hosoi: It's been a long time. Your child has gotten big!

Ogawa: Yes, he is already in junior high. He is giving it his all in his soccer club.

Hosoi: Ah, soccer club? Do you play with him?

Ogawa: Yeah, sometimes. Oh, it's already this time. I've gotta go.

Hosoi: Are you going to take a taxi?

新しい言葉　New Words

☐ お子さん　used to refer to someone else's child

☐ 部(ぶ)　club

☐ こんな　this (used for emphasis)

Dialogues that mix respectful and humble forms

◆ 他の会社からの電話

鈴木： お電話ありがとうございます。TONDAの鈴木でございます。

織田： YAMAHOの織田と申します。お世話になっております。
営業部の佐々木様はいらっしゃいますでしょうか。

鈴木： 申し訳ございません、佐々木はただいま席を外しておりますが。

織田： そうですか。何時ごろお戻りになりますか。

鈴木： 夕方5時ごろに戻るとおもいます。

織田： では、そのころに、あらためてお電話を差し上げます。

鈴木： かしこまりました。そのように申し伝えます。

織田： 失礼いたします。

◆ コンビニ

店員： おはし、スプーンをおつけしますか。

客： はい、お願いします。

店員： 袋にお入れしますか。

客： いえ、いいです。

店員： ポイントカードはお持ちですか。

客： いえ、ないです。

店員： ポイントカード、お作りしますか。

客： いえ、いいです。

◆ ファーストフード

店員： ご注文はお決まりですか？

客： はい、このハンバーガーセット1つお願いします。

店員： ハンバーガーセットおひとつですね。お飲み物は？

客： コーラのMで。

店員： 以上でよろしいですか？

客： はい、いいです。

店員： こちらでお召し上がりですか？

客： いえ、持ち帰りで。

店員： お持ち帰りですね。少々お待ちください。

—A phone call from another company—

Suzuki:	Thank you for calling TONDA. My name is Suzuki.
Oda:	This is Oda from YAMAHO. Thank you for taking my call. Is Mr. Sasaki in the sales department available?
Suzuki:	I'm sorry, Sasaki is away from his desk at the moment.
Oda:	I see. Around what time will he return?
Suzuki:	I believe he'll be back about 5 p.m. this evening.
Oda:	Alright, I'll call again at that time.
Suzuki:	OK. I will let him know.
Oda:	Goodbye.

—At a convenience store—

Employee:	Would you like chopsticks or a spoon?
Customer:	Yes, please.
Employee:	Shall I put your items in a bag?
Customer:	No, I'm fine.
Employee:	Do you have a point card?
Customer:	No, I don't have one.
Employee:	Would you like to create a point card?
Customer:	No thank you.

—At a fast-food restaurant—

Employee:	Have you decided on your order?
Customer:	Yes, I'll have one hamburger set.
Employee:	Alright, one hamburger set. And to drink?
Customer:	With a medium cola.
Employee:	Will that be all?
Customer:	Yes, that's it.
Employee:	And will you be dining here?
Customer:	No, it's to go.
Employee:	OK, takeout. Please wait a moment.

Bikago 美化語

In addition to the respectful and humble forms, Japanese has *bikago* or "beautiful language," which is used to make the speaker come across as refined and elegant. *Bikago* mainly consists of attaching the hiragana characters お and ご to nouns and adjectives.

Although there are many exceptions, a helpful rule of thumb is that お is attached to *wago* (words of Japanese origin), while ご comes before *kango* (words that were originally Chinese). For example, 酒 has two pronunciations: しゅ (Chinese origin) and さけ (Japanese origin). The prefix お is used with さけ, but not with しゅ.

And these are not interchangeable—you can't say おしゅ or ごさけ.

● お＋和語（*wago*）＝ the pronunciation is of Japanese origin

お酒　お体　お顔　お肉　お野菜　お天気　お菓子　お茶碗　お食事　お名前

● ご＋漢語（*kango*）＝ the pronunciation is of Chinese origin

ご飯　ご本　ご気分　ご希望　ご機嫌　ご連絡　ご理解　ご参加

However, some verbs can use either:

お返事・ご返事　　お誕生・ご誕生

● Some words always require お, because they have a totally different meaning without it.

おふくろ *mother*　　おかず *side dish*　　おなか *stomach*

ふくろ *bag*　　かず *numbers*　　なか *inside*

A few words have evolved to customarily have お, so they sound strange without it.

おすし　お箸　お米　お茶

There are also words that cannot come after お or ご, like Western words, places, and disasters.

おコーヒー　　おビール　　お学校　　お市役所　　お火事

Chapter 2

Various Expressions

第2章　いろいろな表現

it happens sometimes

することが（も）ある

> verb dictionary form
> verb nai-form + ことが（も）ある

Point!

- The meaning of することがある is similar to ときどき or たまに.
- However, this pattern implies that it is an unusual event or a rare opportunity.
- Still, it is often used with ときどき or たまに to further clarify the frequency.
- This sounds very similar to ～たことがある; just the tense of the verb preceding こと is different. The use of ta-form in that structure refers to past experience rather than something that is ongoing or in the future.
- The particle も is sometimes used instead of が. Natives might do this because the phrase ことがある can have another unintended meaning (話すことがある can mean I have something I want to talk about), or they may use も simply for emphasis.

例 Ex. ・お酒を飲むことがあります。 *I have a chance to drink alcohol.*

・忙しいと寝ないことがあります。 *I sometimes don't sleep when I'm busy.*

・いつも豚肉をたべますが、牛肉を食べることもあります。
I usually eat pork, but sometimes I eat beef.

（社員食堂で）*(At a company cafeteria)*

あれ、珍しいですね。
Oh, it's rare (to see you here).

ええ、私だって*来ることもありますよ。
Really? I come here once in a while.

いつも愛妻弁当持ってきてるから。
Well, you always bring the lunch box your wife makes.

妻が作らないこともありますから。
Sometimes she doesn't make one.

あっ、ケンカしたんですか〜？
Ah, did you have an argument?

まあ、そういうこともあります。
It happens sometimes.

*だって even

about to; in the middle of; just

するところ　しているところ　したところ

走るところ ➡ 走っているところ ➡ 走ったところ

> verb plain form
> ＋ ところ

Point!

- ところ means *place*, and its usage here shows the *place* in time when the action occurs.
- The tense of the verb before ところ indicates when the action takes place.
- The subject can be anyone, including a third party.

例 Ex.
- ・今から家をでるところです。　*I'm about to leave.*
- ・今、料理を作っているところです。　*I'm in the middle of cooking.*
- ・ちょうど今、帰ったところです。　*I just returned home.*

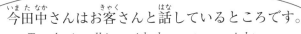
もしもし、そっちの仕事はおわった？
Hey, are you done with the work there?

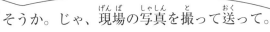
はい、さっき終わって今、現場をでるところです。
Yes, we finished a bit ago and we're about to leave.

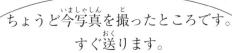
オッケー。ちょっと田中にかわって。
Okay. Let me talk to Tanaka.

今田中さんはお客さんと話しているところです。
Tanaka is talking with the customer right now.

そうか。じゃ、現場の写真を撮って送って。
Oh. Well, take some pictures of the work site and send them to me.

ちょうど今写真を撮ったところです。
すぐ送ります。
I was just about to take some.
I'll send them right away.

71

whether or not

〜かどうか

> verb plain form
> i-adjective plain form
> na-adjective + かどうか
> noun

Point!

- どうか is preceded by a question with a yes or no answer.

  彼は行きますか？　行きませんか？　➡　彼が行くかどうか　＋　わかりません。

  Does he go?　　　Does not he go?　　　whether or not he goes　　　I don't know.

- When the question before どうか ends in んですか (for explanation or emphasis), the ん becomes の.

  彼は行くんですか？＋知ってますか　➡　行くのかどうか知ってますか？

  The standard rules for んです apply here: なのか is used after nouns and na-adjectives.

- どうか is often omitted in conversational Japanese, just as *or not* can be omitted in English.

例 Ex.
- ・今日本が寒いかどうか調べます。

  I'll look up whether Japan is cold or not right now.

- ・息子が元気なのか気になります。

  I'm concerned about whether my son is healthy.

雨の確率は50％だから、降るかどうかわからないね。
There's a 50% chance of rain,
so I don't know whether it will rain or not.

明日のツアー行けるかどうか心配だなあ。
I'm worried whether we can go on the tour today.

そうだね。もし雨だったら、キャンセルできる？
Yeah. If it rains, can we cancel?

うん。無料でキャンセルできるか調べてみるよ。
Yep. I'll try and look up whether we can cancel for free
or not.

I know / I don't know \<statement\>

〜かわかります・〜かわかりません
〜か知っています・〜か知りません

statement ＋か
＋わかります or わかりません

Point!

- The question marker か comes between the first statement and the verb at the end of the sentence.

いつ、彼は帰りましたか ＋ 知っていますか？

➡ いつ彼が帰ったか、知っていますか？

You can't use 知りません for information about yourself. Use わかりません instead.

私 は、明日（私 が）何を食べるか知りません。 ➡ incorrect

明日何を食べるか（まだ）わかりません。 ➡ correct

例 Ex.
・将 来何をするかまだわかりません。
I don't know yet what I'll do in the future.

・夏休みにどこに行くかまだ決めてません。
I still haven't decided where I'll go during summer vacation.

・だれがそんなことを言ったのか知ってますか？
Do you know who said such a thing?

森さんがいつ結婚するか知ってる？
Do you know when Ms. Mori is getting married?

いつか知らない。そろそろお祝い買わないとね。
I don't know when. But we have to buy a gift soon.

そうそう、何あげる？
Right, what should we give her?

まだ何あげるかわからない。
I'm not sure what to give her yet.

森さん、何が好きか知ってる？
Do you know what she likes?

知らない。紅茶が好きかも。いつも飲んでるから。
I don't know. She might like some tea.
She's always drinking it.

Chapter

2

73

supposed to be

〜はず

verb plain form i-adjective na-adjective な noun の	+ はず

Point!

- はず is used for a strong prediction, guess, or expectation that is usually based on evidence.
  In order of certainty:

  犯人_{はんにん}です ➡ 犯人に違_{ちが}いない ➡ 犯人のはず ➡ 犯人かもしれない

- The following adverbs are often used with はず to further specify the level of certainty.

  ぜったい　　きっと　　たぶん　　おそらく

- Use ないはず for negative sentences. ➡ 知_しらないはず

  Sometimes, ない comes after はず to make the statement more forceful. ➡ 知_しってるはずが
  ない。

  This double negative equates to an affirmative statement.

  知らないはずがない ➡ 絶対知_{ぜったいし}っている
  surely doesn't not know ➡ surely knows

例 Ex. ・家族_{かぞく}はみんな寝_ねているはずです。 *I bet my family is asleep.*

・しないはず。 *I don't expect to do that.*

・あの人_{ひと}が犯人_{はんにん}のはず。 *That person must be a criminal.*

森_{もり}さん、そろそろ来_くるはずだけど。どうしたんだろう。
I expected Ms. Mori to be here by now.
I wonder what happened.

そうだね。森_{もり}さんが来_こないはずないよね。
Yeah. There's no way she won't come.

メールしたんでしょ？
You emailed her, right?

したはず。あっ、まだ下書_{したが}きにはいってた！
I thought I did. Ahh, it was still in my drafts!!

どうりで、来_こないはずだよ。*
No wonder, I guess she won't come then.

*This はず shows on the speaker's conviction.

even if ____, I don't mind

——ても、かまいません

> verb te-form ＋も
> i-adjective ＋くても
> na-adjective ＋でも ＋かまいません
> noun ＋でも

Point!

- The verb かまう means *to care*, but it is typically used in this negative form. The English equivalent is *I don't mind* or *Do you mind?*

- nai-form ＋ かまわない ➡ なくてもかまわない it dosen't matter, I don't mind.

  There is a similar expression なくてもいい this English equivalent is *don't need*.

  ——ても　かまいません

  Even if—, I don't mind.

例 Ex.
- ここに座ってもかまいませんか？ *Do you mind if I sit here?*

- いつ来てもかまいませんよ。 *It doesn't matter when you come.*

- 彼女がいなくてもかまわない。 *I don't mind her not being here.*

（コミュニティーセンターの中で） *(At a community center)*

> すみません、ここで子供を遊ばせてもかまいませんか？
> *Excuse me, do you mind if I let my kid play here?*

> かまいませんよ。（子供に）アメたべる？
> *I don't mind at all. (to child) Want some candy?*

> （子供がアメを落とす）
> ああっ、すみません！　ほんとにすみません。
> *(child drops the candy)*
> *Oh, oh! Excuse me! I'm so sorry!*

> そんなにあやまらなくてもいいですよ。
> *No need to apologize so much!*

even though; although

〜ても

> verb te-form ＋ も
> i-adjective ＋ くても
> na-adjective ＋ でも
> noun ＋ でも

Point!

- Just as in English, the statement that follows this pattern is a contrary or opposite result from the statement that precedes it. どんなに or いくら are sometimes added for emphasis.
- いくらですか is used for asking how much something costs, but いくら〜ても means *no matter how*.

例 Ex.

- 日曜日でも 働 きます。　*Even though it's Sunday, I'll work.*

- 暑くてもラーメンが食べたいです。
  Although it's hot, I still want to eat some ramen.

- どんなに 働 いても、お金がたまりません。
  Even though I work and work, I can't save any money.

- いくら辛くても、あきらめません。
  No matter how tough it gets, I won't give up.

最近、日本語の勉 強 がんばってる？
Have you been working hard on your Japanese lately?

うん、でも、いくらがんばっても上 手にならないよ。
Yeah, but no matter how hard I work at it I don't get any better.

そう？ 上 手になってると思うよ。
Really? I think you've gotten good.

話すのはいいけど、漢字はどんなに勉 強 しても忘れちゃう。
Speaking is fine, but I always forget kanji even though I study them.

日本人でも漢字は忘れるよ。
Even Japanese people forget kanji.

ええ、ほんとに？
Wow, seriously?

76

it seems; I hear that; typical of

～らしい

verb plain form	
i-adjective	
na-adjective	＋らしい
noun	

Point!

- らしい translates to *it seems*, which is the same meaning we learned for the sentence ending そうだ in Practical Japanese 2. The difference between the two is this: そうだ indicates that you got the information directly from the source, whereas らしい marks information that you heard secondhand.

  結婚したそうだ。 *I heard she got married.* (heard directly from the bride)
  結婚したらしい。 *I heard she got married.* (heard from someone other than the bride)

- Noun + らしい can also have a different meaning: *just like <noun>* or *typical of <noun>*. The intended meaning can be difficult to parse at first, but the overall tone and context should tell you.

例 Ex.
- 日本は今、寒いらしい。 *I hear it's cold in Japan now.*

- どうやらうまくいかないらしい。 *It seems its not going well somehow.*

- 今日は暖かくて春らしいですね。
  Today is so warm, it feels just like spring.

- あの人は女らしくない。 *That person doesn't act like a typical woman.*

聞きましたか？ 青木さん、辞めるらしいですよ。
Did you hear? It seems Mr. Aoki quit.

えっ、知りませんでした。
最近青木さん、無口で、いつもの青木さんらしくないと思ってました。
Oh, I didn't know.
I did think he's been quiet lately and not like his typical self.

うつ病らしいですよ。
I heard he was depressed.

かわいそうに……。
I feel bad for him...

-ish; like

っぽい

noun ＋ っぽい

Point!

- っぽい has the same meaning as the endings みたい and よう, but it sounds casual and is only attached to nouns. It is often used with colors and some tastes.

  油_{あぶら}っぽい　水_{みず}っぽい　粉_{こな}っぽい　黒_{くろ}っぽい　白_{しろ}っぽい
  oily　　　*watery*　　*powdery*　　*blackish*　　*whitish*

- It can also carry a positive or negative nuance depending on what it describes.

  子供_{こども}っぽい大人_{おとな} ➡ childish adult　　大人_{おとな}っぽい子供_{こども} ➡ adult-like child
  　　　(negative nuance)　　　　　　　　　　　(positive nuance)

例 Ex.
- あの 女_{おんな} の人_{ひと}は 男_{おとこ}っぽいです。　*That woman is manly.*

- このスープ、味_{あじ}が薄_{うす}くて水_{みず}っぽいです。　*This soup is bland and watery.*

- 犯人_{はんにん}は黒_{くろ}っぽい服_{ふく}をきていました。
  The suspect was wearing blackish (dark) clothing.

あれ、今日_{きょう}はなんだか先生_{せんせい}っぽいね。
Woah, you look like a teacher or something today.

ちょっと〜、失礼_{しつれい}じゃない？
先生_{せんせい}っぽい、じゃなくて先生_{せんせい}らしいでしょ。
Hey, isn't that sort of rude?
I don't "look like" a teacher, I am a teacher.

そうだね。本当_{ほんとう}に先生_{せんせい}だからね。
いつも子供_{こども}っぽい服_{ふく}着_きてるけど。
True. You really are a teacher.
But you usually wear clothes that make you look like a kid.

今日_{きょう}は子供_{こども}っぽくないでしょ。
Today I don't look like a kid though.

it seems; looks like; apparently

ようだ・ような・ように

> **verb plain form** ＋よう
> **i-adjective** ＋よう
> **na-adjective** ＋なよう
> **noun** ＋のよう

Point!

- This ending is derived from the noun 様子 (ようす) meaning *state* or *appearance*. It indicates the same thing as みたいだ (see page 117 of Practical Japanese 2), it is just more formal.
- It is used with まるで in the metaphor まるで＿＿＿ようだ (*it is as if ＿＿＿*).
- Be careful not to confuse this ending with the volitional form 〜しよう (*let's do*). The だ at the end is a clue that it isn't volitional: するようだ means *it seems that <someone> is going to ＿＿＿*. It can also be used as a na-adjective (〜ような) or an adverb (〜ように).

例 Ex.
- この部屋にはだれもいないようです。
  It looks like no one is in this room.
- 彼女は、まるで猫のように歩きます。 *She walks as if she is a cat.*
- 春のような天気です。 *This weather feels like spring.*

森さんの結婚式、豪華でしたよ。
Mrs. Mori's wedding ceremony was gorgeous.

相手はどんな人でしたか？
What is her husband like?

イケメンで、まるで俳優のようでしたよ。
森さんもモデルのようにきれいですからね。
*He's really good-looking, almost seems like an actor.
I mean, Mrs. Mori herself is so pretty she looks
like a model.*

そうですね。僕も森さんのような人と結婚したいなあ。
It's true. I'd like to marry someone like her.

to have or exhibit strong feelings of

〜がる、〜がっている

> verb ＋たい＋がる
> i-adjective ＋がる
> na-adjective ＋がる

Point!

- The 〜がる ending is used to describe strong feelings or emotions.

- You can't use it to describe your own feelings, except when it is used as noun（〜がり）meaning *type of person.*

  寒_{さむ}がり　暑_{あつ}がり　怖_{こわ}がり
  person who is always...　*cold*　　*hot*　　*scared*

- It can be combined with たい or ほしい, in which case the final い is dropped.

  アイスクリームを食_たべたがる　　　アイスクリームをほしがる

- This expression sounds direct, so don't use it when speaking to another person about their feelings.

  あなたは食_たべたがっています。　➡　too direct
  あなたは食_たべたいみたいです。　➡　better

例 Ex.
- 彼_{かれ}がトイレに行_いきたがっています。
  He looks like he really has to go to the bathroom.

- 子供_{こども}がおもちゃを欲_ほしがっています。
  The child appears to want the toy badly.

- 彼女_{かのじょ}は犬_{いぬ}を怖_{こわ}がっている。　*She seems very scared of the dog.*

> みきさんが、マイクさんに会_あいたがってたよ。
> *Miki was acting like she wanted to see you.*

> ほんとに？
> ぼくをいやがってるとおもった。
> *Really? It seemed like she didn't like me.*

> どうして？
> *Why?*

> 別_{わか}れる時_{とき}、みきさんはハグしてくれなかったから。
> *When I left, she didn't hug me.*

> みきさんは恥_はずかしがり屋_や*だからね。
> マイクさんが帰_{かえ}ってから寂_{さび}しがってたよ。
> *She's just a shy type of person.*
> *After you left, she seemed sad.*

*屋_や is often attached after 〜がり→がりや

there is a smell / sound / taste

におい・音・味　がする

> sensory noun ＋がする

Point!

- This pattern expresses that the speaker has noticed a sensation such as a smell（におい）, sound（おと）, taste（あじ）, or feeling（かんじ）.
- A word or phrase will precede the sensory noun to describe the sensation.
- The particle が is always used here. Be careful not to confuse this with にする (see next page).

例 Ex.
- 間違ってる感じがします。　*I feel like this is wrong.*
- ドアをたたく音がしました。　*There was knock at the door.*
- このスープは魚の味がしますね。　*This soup tastes like fish.*

ねえ、なんかいい匂いがするね。
Hey, something smells good.

ホントだ。なんだろう。焼き肉かな？
Yeah, it does. I wonder what it is. Barbecued meat?

隣の家から匂いがするよ。
The smell is coming from the neighbor's house.

わいわい騒いでる声もするし、
焼き肉パーティーかな。
It's noisy over there too, so they might be having a barbecue.

Chapter 2

to decide to; to make or be

〜にする・〜くする

> i-adjective (ku-form) ＋する
> na-adjective ＋にする
> noun ＋にする

Point!

- This pattern can be used to indicate a decision that is made.
- When used with adjectives, it can also mean to make or to be:

部屋をきれいにする　　明るくする
make the room clean　*be cheerful*
(clean the room)

例 Ex.
- ミーティングは明日にしましょう。
  Let's decide to have the meeting tomorrow.

- 人にやさしくしたほうがいいですよ。
  It's better to be kind to people.

- しずかにしてください。　*Please be quiet.*

何にする？
What will you have?

わたし、甘口にする。
I'll go with the mild one.

俺は辛口にしよう。
すみません。辛口と甘口を一つずつお願いします。
I think I'll get the spicy.
Excuse me. One mild and one spicy, please.

（一口食べる）あれ、甘すぎる。
すみません。ちょっと辛くしてください。
(takes a bite) Oh, this is too mild.
Sorry, please make this a little spicier.

to continue to; to come to

〜ていく・〜てくる

$$\text{verb te-form} + \begin{array}{l} くる \\ きた \\ いく \\ いった \end{array}$$

Point!

- This pattern is used when something is moving or changing over time. 〜てくる shows that the object or state is approaching the speaker (either physically or temporally), while 〜ていく shows that it is moving away from the speaker.

- It is formed by adding いく or くる to the te-form of a verb. These endings are almost always written in kana rather than kanji, and the resulting pattern is treated as a single word.

- The pattern is often used with other words that indicate change, such as:

これから	だんだん	どんどん
from now on	*gradually*	*quickly*

Chapter

2

例 Ex.
- 日本語がだんだんわかってきました。
  I've gradually come to understand Japanese.

- これから人口が減っていきます。
  The population will continue to decline from now on.

だんだんあったかくなってきたね。
It's gradually gotten warmer, hasn't it?

3月だから。どんどんあったかくなっていくよ。
Because its March. It will continue to warm up quickly now.

あれ、何かこっちに飛んでくる。UFO?
Hey, something is flying this way. A UFO?

どこどこ？
Where, where?

もう飛んで行ったよ。
It already flew away.

before; after

まえ（に）・あと（で）

> verb dictionary form ＋ まえ
> verb ta-form ＋ あと
> noun の ＋ まえ/あと

Point!

- The dictionary form of a verb is used with まえ, while ta-form is used with あと. Unlike in English, these tenses don't change to match the tense of the verb at the end of the sentence.

  家に帰ったあと、テレビをみる。 ➡ *After I go home, I'll watch TV.*

  Note that 帰った is past tense even though the overall sentence describes something in the future.

- The particle て acts similar to the te-form of a verb. That's why it is used with あと—the action that precedes it must occur prior to the one that comes after, just like when te-form is used to connect two verbs. Since まえ is the opposite (the second action occurs first), it uses the particle に.

例 Ex.
- 学校に行くまえに、宿題をしました。
  Before I went to school, I did my homework.
- 仕事のまえに、メールをチェックしないといけません。
  I have to check my email before work.
- 食事のあと、歯みがきをしましょう。 *I brush my teeth after I eat.*
- またあとで、はなしましょう。 *Let's talk more later.*

マイクさん、日本に来たあと、日本語勉強したの？
So Mike, you studied Japanese after coming to Japan?

日本に来るまえに、学校で日本語を勉強したんだ。
I studied Japanese at school before coming to Japan.

ああ、だから上手なんだね。アメリカに帰ったあとどうするの？
Oh, that's why you're good at it. What will you do after returning to America?

帰ったあと、また学校にいくつもり。
仕事したいけど、資格がないからいい仕事ができない。
After I return, I plan to go to school again. I want to work, but I can't find a good job because I don't have any qualifications.

資格をとったあとで、仕事を探したほうがいいよね。
I guess it's better to look for work after getting some qualifications.

only; as many as

だけ・しか〜ない・も

> noun ＋ だけ / しか〜ない
> number ＋ も

Point!

- These words are used for emphasis.
  When も comes after a number, it emphasizes that it is a large amount.
  100個もある！ ➡ *There's 100 of them!*

- だけ and しか〜ない both mean only, but the former has a positive nuance and the latter has a negative nuance.

  手数料は100円だけです。　　　今100円しか持っていない。
  The fee is only ¥100.　　　*I only have ¥100 right now.*

例 Ex.
- 私だけプレゼントをもらえました。　*Only I received a present.*

- 今日は、お客さんが10人しか来ませんでした。
  Only 10 customers came today.

- 甘いケーキを5個も食べてしまいました！
  I ate as many as 5 sweet cakes!

今日、ドーナツを20個も買っちゃった。
I bought 20 donuts today.

20個も!?　どうして？
20!? Why?

安かったから。今日だけ1個100円だったんだよ。
たくさん食べてね！
They were cheap. Just for today they were only ¥100 each.
Eat up!

お腹いっぱいで1個しか食べられないよ。
I'm full, so I can only eat one.

Chapter 2

85

come to do; become able to

〜ようになる

> verb dictionary form＋ようになる
> verb nai-form＋ようになる
> verb potential form＋ようになる

> **Point!**

- The verb なる means to *become*. This pattern denotes something that you didn't or couldn't do before, but now you do or can do.

  When used with potential form: できるようになった ➡ now I can do it (but I couldn't before)

  When used with dictionary form: するようになった ➡ now I do it (I was able to before but didn't)

- Although 〜ようになる can be used with the nai-form of a verb, 〜なくなる is more common.

  食べないようになった ➡ uncommon　　食べなくなった ➡ common

例 Ex.
- 赤ちゃんが話せるようになりました。*The baby became able to speak.*
- 漢字が読めるようになったけど、書けるようになりません。
  I can now read kanji, but I still can't write them.
- 大学生になって、一人で買い物するようになりました。
  After becoming a college student, I started going shopping on my own.

日本語がペラペラ話せるようになったね。
You've become able to speak Japanese well.

ありがとう。でも、敬語はまだ難しい。
Thanks. But keigo is still difficult for me.

日本人にも敬語は難しいよ。
Keigo is difficult even for Japanese people.

いつから上手に話せるようになったの？
When did you become able to use it correctly?

就職して、たくさん使うようになってからだね。
When I got a job and came to use it a lot there.

try to do; make sure to do

〜ようにする

> verb dictionary form ＋ ようにする
> verb nai-form ＋ ようにする

Point!

- ようになる describes the state of something, while 〜ようにする indicates the speaker's will. And unlike 〜ようになる, nai-form is often used with this pattern; it is quite common to say 〜ないようにする.

- The patterns 〜ようにしましょう and 〜ようにしてください are used to make someone aware of something they should or shouldn't do.

例 Ex.
・これから、単語を毎日10個おぼえるようにします。
From now on, I'm going to try to memorize 10 words every day.

・お酒をあまり飲まないようにしています。
I'm trying not to drink much alcohol.

・データは削除しないようにしてください。
Please try not to delete the data.

いつも元気ですね。
You're always full of energy.

最近毎日運動するようにしてるんだ。
それから青汁をのむようにしてる。
*I've been making sure to exercise every day lately.
And I'm trying to drink more vegetable juice.*

青汁ですか。
わたしも飲むようにしようかな。
*Vegetable juice?
Maybe I should try to drink some.*

効果があるよ。
It does have an effect.

in order to

ように・ために

> potential form or nai-form ＋ように
> intransitive verb ＋ように
> dictionary form ＋ために
> transitive verb ＋ために

Point!

- Both ように and ために mark the purpose or reason that something is done, but there is a difference: ように indicates that the goal is somewhat more difficult to achieve.

忘れないようにメモをしておく。 ➡ don't say 忘れないために

I'll write a memo so I don't forget.

- The verb forms that precede each pattern are also different; ように is used with potential, nai-form, and intransitive verbs, while ために is paired with dictionary form and transitive verbs.

例 Ex.
- 日本語が話せるように勉強する。

  I'll study Japanese so that I can speak it.

- 友達と話すために喫茶店に行った。

  I went to the coffee shop to speak with my friend.

- ドアが閉まるように直した。 *I fixed the door so that it will close.*

- ドアを閉めるために立ち上がった。 *I stood up to close the door.*

マイクさんはどうして日本に来たの？
Mike, why did you come to Japan?

日本語を勉強するために来たんだ。
いつか日本で働きたいから。
I came to study Japanese.
I'd like to work in Japan someday.

日本で働けるようにがんばってね！
何かあったら、このメアドに連絡して。
Well, study hard so you can get a job in Japan!
If you need anything, contact me at this email address.

ありがとう。失くさないように、今すぐ登録するよ。
Thanks. I'll save it right now so I don't lose it.

I hope

〜ように。

verb masu-form＋ように。
verb potential form＋ように。

Point!

- This pattern is used to indicate something the speaker hopes will happen.
- Always use ます form before this sentence-ending ように。
- When potential form is used, it's usually for positive statements.
- Don't confuse this pattern with 〜といいです (see page 27).

例 Ex.
- ・大学に合格できますように。 *I hope that I can get into university.*
- ・お金持ちになれますように。 *I hope you can become rich.*
- ・台風が来ませんように。 *I hope that the typhoon doesn't come here.*
- ・病気になりませんように。 *I hope you don't get sick.*

（神社で）（*At a shrine*）

ここにお金をいれて、お願いをするんだよ。
You put the money in here, then make a wish.

わかりました。じゃあ…
（みかさんと結婚できますように…）
I see. Well, then...
(I hope that Mika and I can get married...)

すごく真剣にお願いしてたね。
なにお願いしたの？
That was very serious. What did you wish for?

いや、はずかしいから…。
Oh, I'm embarassed to say...

Chapter **2**

as; for; representing

として・としては

noun ＋として・としては

Point!

- として is used to express one's role or position or to indicate that something is representative of a group.

  私は英語教師として日本に来ました。 ⇒ *I came to Japan as an English teacher.*

- If は is attached to this pattern （としては）, it contrasts the preceding noun with something else.

  Xとしてはいいけど、Yとしては良くない。 ⇒ *It's good for X, but not good for Y.*

例 Ex.
・兄は学校の代表としてスピーチをします。
  My older brother will give a speech representing our school.

・子供にとって留学はいいと思いますが、親としては心配です。
  Studying abroad might be good for a child, but as a parent it is a cause for worry.

・渋谷は、遊ぶところとしてはいいけど、住むところとしてはあまり良くないです。
  Shibuya is nice for going out and having fun, but it's not so great as a place to live.

本多選手が日本人代表としてオリンピックに出るらしいよ。
I heard Honda is going to represent Japan in the Olympics.

へえ、今外国のチームにいるけど、オリンピックは日本人として出るんだね。
Really? So he's playing on an overseas team now, but he's going to appear as a Japanese player in the Olympics.

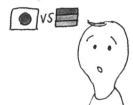

うん、ぼくは日本人として日本を応援するけど実は、ドイツのチームがすき。
As a Japanese person I want to support Japan, but I actually like the German team.

for (unexpected)

にしては

> verb plain form＋にしては
> noun＋にしては

┌─ **Point!** ─┐

- にしては describes a state that is different from what is expected.

- Don't confuse this with してはいけません。Always use the particle に.

- There is a similar expression to this: わりには. The difference between them comes down to specificity—わりには can be preceded by a more generic word, while the word that comes before にしては needs to be more specific.

年のわりには元気です。　　　　８０才にしては元気です。

She's energetic for her age.　　*She's energetic for 80 years old.*

例 Ex.　・冬にしては気温が高いですね。　*This is a high temperature for winter.*

・平日にしては、道路が混んでいます。

There's a lot of traffic for a weekday.

・（いつも早く来るのに）林さんにしては、遅いです。

This is late for Mr. Hayashi (because he always comes early).

・初めて日本に来たにしては、日本語が上手ですね。

For the first time being in Japan, your Japanese is good.

> この間、英単語のアプリ見つけたんだけど、
> Level 1 にしては難しいんだよね。
> *The other day I found an app for learning English words,*
> *but this is hard for Level 1.*

> どれ、みせて。ああ、ほんとだ。
> でも無料にしては、いいと思うよ。
> *Which one, let me see. Oh, you're right.*
> *But it's good for a free app.*

> たしかに。無料で使えるにしては
> よくできてるよ。
> *Definitely. It's well-made for something*
> *you can use for free.*

even though

にしても

> verb plain form ＋にしても
> adjective ＋にしても
> noun ＋にしても

Point!

- This expression is used between a statement of truth and the speaker's opinion.
- It is sometimes used when the speaker wants to express a critical opinion.
- Don't confuse this with ～くても：

暑くても頑張る。 　　　　　　　　暑いにしても暑すぎる。

Even though it's hot, I'll try my best. 　　*I know it's hot, but this is too hot.*

例 Ex.
- お金がないにしても、100円くらいはあります。

  I don't have any money—well, I have 100 yen, actually.

- 悪気がなかったにしても、人の悪口はいけません。

  Even though you didn't have ill intentions, you shouldn't speak bad about other people.

- 忙しいにしても、10分くらいは話せるでしょう。

  Even though I'm busy, I suppose I can talk for ten minutes or so.

- 社長にしても、この問題は難しいです。

  Even though he's the company president, this is a tricky problem.

電車来るの遅くない？
Isn't the train running late?

あ、今アナウンスで事故があって遅れるって。
Oh, there was an announcement just now saying that it would be late due to an accident.

そうだったんだ。それにしても遅いね。
もう15分も待ってるよ。
Is that what happened?
Even so, it's late. We've already been waiting 15 minutes.

15ふんも！

そうだね。遅れるにしても、遅すぎるよね。
Yeah. I know they said it would be delayed, but this is too slow.

for (usage)

用・向け

noun＋用
noun＋向け

Point!

- The kanji 用（よう）is attached to nouns to show that something exists for the benefit or use of those nouns.

- In English, this is often expressed using a possessive apostrophe:

  子供用の部屋　　女性用ハンドバッグ

  room for kids　　*women's handbag*

- 向け is similar to 用, the difference being one of exclusivity.

  子供用　➡　only children can use it

  子供向け　➡　intended for children, but adults can also use it

例 Ex. ・子供用のいすがありますか？　*Do you have a chair for children?*

・仕事用と私用のメールアドレスがあります。

I have a business email and a personal email.

・こちらは年配の方向けの家です。　*This house is suited for elderly people.*

・外国人向けのツアーを探しています。

I'm trying to find a tour for foreigners.

彼女にお土産買いたいからつきあって。
I want to buy a souvenir for my girlfriend, so come with me.

いいよ。この店はたくさん女性用のものがあるよ。
Sure. This store has a lot of things for souvenirs.

これは子供用？ 女性用なの？ 何に使うの？
Is this intended for kids? Would it be good for a girl?

それは意味ないよ。飾るため。
I think it would be fine for either.

日本らしいから、これにするよ。
すみません、これ、プレゼント用にお願いします。
It reminds me of Japan, so I'll get it.
Excuse me, I'd like to purchase this for a present.

instead of; in place of

かわりに

verb plain form ＋かわりに
noun ＋のかわりに

Point!

● In most cases, かわりに simply means *instead of*. But it sometimes serves a different function within a sentence:

土曜日に学校に行った代わりに、月曜日が休みになりました。

Since we had school on Saturday, we have Monday off.

例 Ex. ・ペンを使うかわりに鉛筆を使いました。 *I used a pencil instead of a pen.*

・ダイエットのために、ご飯を食べる代わりにスムージーを飲みます。
For my diet, I drink a smoothie instead of eating a meal.

・牛乳の代わりに水を使ってパンケーキが作れますよ。
You can make pancakes using water instead of milk.

・先生は赤ちゃんができました。そのかわりに他の先生が来ました。
My teacher had a baby. Another teacher came in her place.

明日って図書館休み？
Is the library closed tomorrow?

ううん、休みじゃないよ。祝日だから開いてるよ。
No, it's not closed. It's a national holiday, so it's open.

休館日だけど祝日だから開いてるの？
*It's normally closed on that day of the week,
but now it's open because of the national holiday?*

そう、そのかわりに次の日が休みになるんだよ。
*Right, which means that it will be closed
on the following day.*

じゃ、私のかわりに本を返してくれない？私、明日バイトなの。
*Well, can you return this book for me?
I have to work at my part-time job tomorrow.*

え。
Oh.

about; regarding

について

noun ＋ について

┌─ **Point!** ─┐

● について means *about* or *regarding*, but unlike English it comes after the word or phrase it marks.

日本文化について　　　　　昨日のニュースについて
about Japanese culture　　　*regarding yesterday's news*

● This expression is often attached to こと, which translates literally as *thing(s)*. In this case, there is a nuance of referring to specific items within the topic.

日本文化のことについて
about Japanese cultural things

● こと can also be used without について to mean *about* in some situations.

あなたのことが心配です。
I'm worried about you.

例 Ex. ・日本の歴史について調べています。　*I'm learning about Japan's history.*

Chapter
2

論文の課題ってなんだっけ？
What was our report about again?

日本の伝統文化についてだよ。
It's about the traditional culture of Japan.

伝統文化についてか〜。
サブカルチャーについてなら、たくさんかけるのになあ。
About traditional culture...
If only it was about subcultures,
we would have lots to write about.

ほんとだよな。ゲームとかアニメのこととか。
100年もたてばもう伝統になるかもね。
Isn't that the truth. About stuff like video games and anime.
A hundred years from now,
that might be the traditional culture.

thanks to; because of; on account of

おかげで・せいで

> verb plain form ＋ おかげ・せい
> i-adjective ＋ おかげ
> na-adjective ＋ なおかげ
> noun ＋ のおかげ

Point!

- In English, the phrase *thanks to* <noun> can have either a positive or a sarcastically negative meaning.
- おかげで expresses the positive meaning of *thanks to*.
- せいで expresses the negative meaning of *thanks to* (the word せい means *fault* or *cause*).
- These patterns can also come at the end of a sentence.
  おかげです　　せいです

例 Ex.

・先生のおかげで大学に合格できました。
Thanks to my teacher, I was able to get into university.

・努力したおかげで漢字が読めるようになりました。
Thanks to all that hard work, I can now read kanji.

・事故のせいで電車が遅れました。 *The train was late thanks to an accident.*

・遅刻したせいで先生に怒られました。
My teacher got mad at me because I was late.

受験のせいで
高校3年の時はぜんぜん楽しくなかったな。
Thanks to the entrance exam, our third year of high school was no fun at all.

でも努力したおかげで大学に入れたでしょ。
But we got into college thanks to our hard work.

そうだね。がんばって勉強したおかげでだいぶ英単語覚えたし。
ただそのせいで、話すのは苦手かな。
True. We learned a lot of English words on account of all that studying. But because of that, we can't really speak it well.

たしかに。そのせいで、
話すのが苦手な人が多いよね。
Yep. A lot of people are in the same situation due to the way Japanese is used to teach English.

Chapter 3

Conjunctions and Adverbs

第3章　接続詞と副詞

> So far, we've learned how to connect nouns, adjectives, and verbs.

noun + noun	と	ex) コーヒーと紅茶
adjective + adjective	て / で	ex) 大きくて白い / しずかでやさしい
verb + verb	て form	ex) 朝起きて、水を飲みます。

> Now, let's look at how to connect entire sentences!

Parallel and そして・それから

そして and それから are used to connect sentences.

富士山 はきれいな山です。そして有名です。
富士山 はきれいな山だね。それから、有名だね。

Mt. fuji is a beautiful mountain. And it is famous.

> そして sounds more formal than それと and それから.

Addition besides; plus それに・それと・それから・そして

それと is commonly used to mean *besides*, but それに and それから can work as well.

スーパーで野菜を買わないといけません。それに、牛乳も買わないといけません。

I have to buy some vegetables at the supermarket. Plus, I need to buy some milk.

> わたし、パスタとサラダにする。それからケーキ。
> *I'll have pasta and a salad. And some cake.*

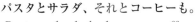

> パスタとサラダ、それとコーヒーも。
> *Pasta and salad, plus some coffee.*

These can also be used to connect nouns.

Addition (emphasis)　also, furthermore　そのうえ・しかも・さらに ……

そのうえ sounds formal, so it is used in phrases like the one below.

森さんにはお世話になりました。そのうえ、お土産までいただいて、本当にすみません。
Thank you for everything, Mr. Mori. And I also feel bad that you went to the trouble of getting me a souvenir.

しかも is used quite often in conversation.

今日は仕事がたくさんあります。しかも銀行までいかないと！
I have a ton of work today. And on top of that, I have to go all the way to the bank!

さらに generally means *further* or *furthermore*. When used with numbers or quantities, it indicates an increase or decrease. It is used in both formal and informal conversation.

さらに気温は上がっていくでしょう。
The temperature is probably going to rise even further.

コーヒーを5杯飲んで、さらに、夜1杯飲んじゃった。
I drank 5 cups of coffee, then I even drank another cup at night.

Time　(and) then　そして・それから・それで・で ………………………

As we saw before, そして is more formal than それから.

6時に仕事が終わりました。そして、友達に会いました。
仕事6時に終わったよ。それから、友達に会った。

I got off work at 6. Then I met my friend.

それで・て are used to urge the speaker on or to continue an idea.

昨日、車が壊れちゃって。
My car broke down yesterday.

それで？（どうしたの）
And?
(what did you do about it)

で、近くの修理工場に電話したんだ。
And so I called a nearby repair shop.

Result so; that's why そういうわけで・だから・それで ·····················

We've learned that から・だから and ので・なので can be used after noun, verbs, or adjectives. Although you can't begin a sentence with から, ので, or なので at the beginning of the sentence, young people are starting to use なので in this way.

そういうわけで sounds a little more formal than the other expressions. The word わけ means reason, while そういう refers to the previous sentence.

> きのうから高い熱がありまして。そういうわけで、今日はお休みさせてください。
>
> *I've had a high fever since yesterday. That's why I'd like to take the day off.*

だから and それで are more casual.

> きのうお腹がいたくて。だから、なんにも食べられなかった。
>
> *My stomach hurt yesterday. So I wasn't able to eat anything.*
>
> あ、それで元気なかったんだね？
>
> *Oh, so that's why you had no energy?*

Starting / ending conversation Well (then) ·····························

それでは、では、じゃあ・さて

> それでは・では、会議を始めましょう。
>
> *Well then, let's begin the meeting.*
>
> じゃ、終わりにしようか。
>
> *Well, let's end here?*
>
> さて、行きましょうか。
>
> *Well, shall we go?*

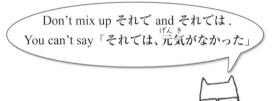

Don't mix up それで and それでは .
You can't say 「それでは、元気がなかった」

Describing steps of a process first; next; then; finally ·············

first	next; then	finally
まず・はじめに・最初に	そして・それから	おわりに・最後に

Although there are multiple words you can use to describe chronological order, there isn't a significant difference between them.

> ① まず、電源を押してください。
>
> *First, press this power button.*
>
> ② それから、運転を選んでください。
>
> *Next, select the mode of operation.*
>
> ③ 最後に、温度を設定してください。
>
> *Finally, set the temperature.*

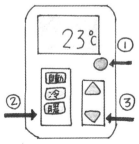

Achievement　finally; at last　ようやく・やっと

ようやく and やっと are used to express the achievement of something. やっと is more colloquial than ようやく.

> ようやく、長い論文を書き終わりました。
> やっと、長い論文、書き終わったよ。
> *I finally finished writing this long essay.*

These words can also indicate a long wait for something.

> ようやく春が来ましたね。　　ええ、ようやくですね。
> *Spring is finally here.*　　*Yes, at last.*
>
> 校長先生の話長かったな～　　うん、やっと終わったよ。
> *Man, the principal's speech was long...*　　*Yeah, he finally finished.*

Result　finally　とうとう・ついに

とうとう and ついに are used for both positive and negative results. They are seen in both formal and informal speech.

> ５年もかかって、とうとう新しいビルが完成しました。　　Happy
> *After five long years, the new building is finally complete.*
> ５０年後、とうとう古いビルは壊されてしまいました。　　Sad
> *Fifty years later, the old building was finally demolished.*

とうとう focuses on time, whereas, ついに emphasizes the result itself.

> ついに新しいビルが完成しました！
> *The new building is finally complete!*

Result　ultimately, in the end　けっきょく

けっきょく is used when describing results in both formal and informal speech.

> 試合の結果は、けっきょく、引き分けになりました。
> *In the end, the match resulted in a tie.*
>
> 迷ったけど、けっきょく行かないことにしました。
> *I was undecided, but I ultimately decided not to go.*

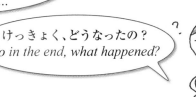

> えーと、最初に僕がおもちゃで遊んでて、
> それでお兄ちゃんが来て、それで…。
> *Um, at first I was playing with a toy,*
> *then brother came, and...*

> けっきょく、どうなったの？
> *So in the end, what happened?*

Same result　anyway; either way　とにかく・どうせ

青い靴と赤い靴、どっちがいいかな？
Which is better, the blue shoes or the green shoes?

どっちでもいいよ。とにかく急がないと！
Either is fine. Anyway, we have to hurry!

どうせ sometimes has a pessimistic nuance.

どうせがんばっても、無理ですよ。どうせ私なんか…。
Even if I try my best, it's impossible anyway. Either way, I'm just…

Changing topics　by the way　ところで

こんにちは。今日はいい天気ですね。
Hello. Nice weather today, isn't it?

ええ、ほんとに。ところで、この間の話ですが…。
Yes, it really is. By the way,
about our discussion the other day…

Bringing up a similar top　speaking of that　そういえば・と言えば

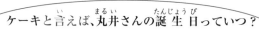

このケーキ、おいしいね。
This cake is good.

ケーキと言えば、丸井さんの誕生日っていつ？
Speaking of cake, when is Marui's birthday?

そういえば、もうすぐだよね。
Now that you mention it, it's soon.

Extra information　by the way; for your information　ちなみに

Battery って日本語でなんて言いますか？
How do you say "battery" in Japanese?

乾電池です。
ちなみに乾電池は日本人が発明したらしいですよ。
"Kandenchi." By the way, I heard that batteries were invented
by a Japanese person.

Examples for example 例えば

京都には有名なお寺がたくさんあります。例えば、金閣寺や清水寺などです。

There are many famous temples in Kyoto. For example, Kinkaku-ji and Kiyomizu-dera.

例 can also be used as noun meaning *example*. In this case, the kanji is the same but the pronunciation is different.

すみません、例をください。
Sorry, please give an example.

Emphasis especially; particularly 特に

私の趣味は映画をみることです。特にアクション映画が大好きです。

Watching movies is a hobby of mine. I especially love action films.

Summing up or rephrase in other words つまり、〜ということです。

明日からゴールデンウィークです。つまり、連休ということです。
Golden Week starts tomorrow. In other words, consecutive days off.

昨日は忙しかったし、おなかがいたかったし…。
I was busy yesterday, and my stomach hurt...

つまり宿題はしてないということですね。
In other words, you didn't do your homework.

Contrary rather than; not really というより・というか・ていうか

私はお金持ちになりたいというより、幸せになりたいんです。
Rather than being rich, I just want to be happy.

どうしたの？ 悲しいの？
What happened? Are you feeling sad?

うん…ていうかさびしい。
Yeah...not really sad, but lonely.

The set phrase なんというか (or なんていうか) is used when you aren't sure how to explain something.

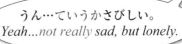

なんというか…
How should I say it...

Choice A or B   or; or else また は・それとも・それか

または and それとも are formal.

　　コーヒーはお食事の前にしますか？　または（それとも）お食事の後にしますか？

　　Should we have some coffee before our meal? Or after the meal?

それか is informal.

　　コーヒー？　それか紅茶？　*Coffee? Or some tea?*

あの電車にのる？
Get on that train?

そうだね。あれか、次の電車。
Yeah. That, or the next train.

これか or あれか can also be used depending on the situation.

But you can't say これとも or あれとも.

A but B   however; but; still しかし・が・でも・ところが

しかし is formal and used at the beginning of a sentence.

　　日本は小さい国です。しかし、人口が多いです。（formal speech）

　　Japan is a small country. However, it has a large population.

でも is more casual than しかし, but otherwise has the same meaning.

　　日本は小さい国だよ。でも、人口が多いんだ。

　　Japan is small. But it has a lot of people.

が is usually used in the middle of a sentence.

　　日本は小さい国ですが、人口が多いです。

だが is used after nouns and na-adjectives. This is more literary and formal than しかし or でも.

　　日本は小さい国だが、人口が多い。　　日本は小さいが、人口が多い。

ところが indicates that the following statement is unexpected. It is used more in writing than conversation.

　　朝は、とてもいい天気でした。ところが、午後は雪が降ってきました。

　　The weather was splendid this morning. Still, it snowed in the afternoon.

Regret or surprise **even though** のに・なのに・ても ·····················

のに is used after verbs and i-adjectives. なのに is used after nouns and na-adjectives.
These patterns express the surprise of the speaker.

お腹がいたいのに、アイスクリーム食べたんですか?!

Even though your stomach hurts, you ate some ice cream?!

Since this pattern indicates that something is unexpected, it can't be used to express
a person's will.

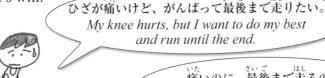

ひざが痛いけど、がんばって最後まで走りたい。
*My knee hurts, but I want to do my best
and run until the end.*

痛いのに、最後まで走るの?
*Run until the end even though your knee
hurts?*

のに can also show that the speaker is upset.

せっかく料理をつくったのに、だれも食べなかった!

Even though I went to the trouble of cooking, no one ate!

The te-form pattern ~ても also means *even though*, but it isn't as emotionally
forceful as のに.

働く ➡ 働いても   急ぐ ➡ 急いでも

がんばって働いても、お金持ちになれない。

Even though I work hard, I can't get rich.

急いでも、バスに間に合わない。

Even though I hurry, I still miss the bus.

Adjectives conjugate like this:

暑い ➡ 暑くても   ひま ➡ ひまでも

When these patterns come at the beginning of a sentence, use それ to refer to the
previous sentence.

がんばって働きました。それなのに、お金持ちになれません。

I worked so hard. But even with that, I couldn't become rich.

急いだよ。それでも、バスに間に合わなかったんだよ。

I hurried. But even so, I still missed the bus.

There are many adverbs ending in り, but let's look at some of the more common ones. These words can sound very similar, so it is helpful to memorize them using entire phrases rather than lists of single words.

ゆっくり　はっきり　たっぷり　ぐっすり　うっかり　しっかり　すっきり　のんびり

■ **ゆっくり**　*slowly*

ゆっくり話してください。　*Please speak slowly.*

おそく is not used for this meaning because おそい has a negative nuance of being late.

今日はすごくつかれた。　　ゆっくり休んでね。
I'm really tired today.　　*Take it easy now.*

■ **たっぷり**　*a lot*

たっぷり食べました。　*I ate a lot.*

■ **ぐっすり**　*deeply; tight*

ぐっすり寝ました。　*I slept deeply.*

■ **はっきり**　*clearly*

はっきりわかりました。　*I understand clearly.*

もごもご……
<mumble mumble>

はっきり言ってよ。
Speak clearly.

■ **うっかり**　*carelessly*

うっかり忘れました。　*I carelessly forgot.*

■ **しっかり**　*firmly; properly*

一日三回、しっかり食べましょう。

We should eat three proper meals a day.

しっかりして！
Get a hold of yourself!

■ **すっきり**　*refreshed*

シャワーをあびて、すっきりしました。　*I felt refreshed after taking a shower.*

■ **のんびり**　*relaxed; carefree*

休みなので、うちでのんびりします。

I have the day off, so I'm going to relax at home.

きみはいつものんびりした人だね。
You're the type of person who's always taking it easy, aren't you?

そう？
Oh?

と adverbs

There are also adverbs that end in と.

わざと　きちんと/ちゃんと　そっと　ほっと　じっと

■ **わざと**　*on purpose; intentionally*
わざとじゃないんです。　*It wasn't intentional.*

■ **きちんと/ちゃんと**　*properly; neatly*
きちんと（ちゃんと）すわりなさい。　*Sit up properly.*
クツはちゃんとそろえてね。　*Arrange your shoes neatly.*

■ **そっと**　*carefully*
危ないから、そっと扱ってください。
It's dangerous, so please handle it carefully.

■ **ほっと（する）**　*relieved*
母の病気が治って、ほっとしました。
I'm relieved that my mother recovered from her illness.

■ **じっと**　*quietly; motionlessly*
男の子は、いつもじっとしていません。
That boy just won't sit still.

■ **じっとみる**　*stare fixedly*
あの男の人、私をじっとみていてこわい。
That man is staring at me and scaring me.

■ **さっと・さっさと**　*quickly*
男の人は、おばあさんが来ると、さっと立ち上がりました。
The man stood up quickly when an old woman approached.

さっさとやっちゃおう！　*Let's get it done quickly!*

* Sometimes と is added to り adverbs emphasize the adverb.

のんびりとする　　　ぐっすりとねむる
really relax　　　*sleep really deeply*

Amount　たくさん・いっぱい・すこし・ちょっと

■ **たくさん（の）**　*a lot*
東京はいつもたくさん人がいます。　*There's always a lot of people in Tokyo.*

■ **いっぱい**　*full*

幸せで胸がいっぱいです。
I'm so happy, my heart feels full.

■ **すこし**　*a little*
少しお時間ありますか？　*Do you have a minute?*

■ **ちょっと**　*a little bit (casual)*
さとうをちょっと入れてくれる？　*Can you add a little bit of sugar?*

* すこし and ちょっと can be used with だけ and しか (page 85).
少ししかありません。　　ちょっとだけ入れてください。
There's only a little.　Please add just a little more.

Change　だんだん・どんどん・ますます・だいぶ・ずいぶん

■ **だんだん**　*gradually*
だんだんあったかくなってきましたね。　*It's gradually gotten warmer, hasn't it.*

■ **どんどん**　*quickly*
子供はどんどん大きくなります。
Children grow up so quickly.

■ **ますます**　*increasingly*
前から、日本語がじょうずでしたけど、ますます上手になりましたね。
Your Japanese was good before, but it has gotten better and better.

■ **だいぶ**　*greatly; mostly*
たくさん宿題があったけど、だいぶ終わりました。
I had a lot of homework, but it's mostly finished.
だいぶ体の具合がよくなったよ。　*My physical condition is greatly improved.*

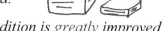

■ **ずいぶん**　*rather; quite; considerably*
あんなに小さかったのに、ずいぶん大きくなりましたね。
Even though it was so small before, its grown considerably.

* ずいぶん has the same meaning as とても and すごく, but it is often used with verbs that indicate change (なる, ふえる, etc.).

ものすごく・めっちゃ・じゅうぶん・非常に・かなり / けっこう・だいたい・ほとんど

■ **じゅうぶん**　*enough; sufficient; plenty*

じゅうぶん休んだので、元気になりました。
I got plenty of rest, so I feel better now.

■ **非常に**　*extremely; extraordinarily*

This is stronger and more formal than とても and すごく.

非常に感心いたしました。　*I am extremely impressed by you.*

■ **めっちゃ**　*very*

Although this word is from the Osaka dialect, it is very popular in other places as well.

めっちゃうれしい！　　めっちゃいい！
I'm so happy!　　　　*This is totally great!*

There is also the word めちゃくちゃ which means *messy*.

部屋がめちゃめちゃ ➡ *the room is messy*

■ **かなり、けっこう**　*quite; pretty*

あの人の日本語はネイティブにかなり近いですよ。
That person's Japanese is quite close to that of a native.

■ **だいたい、ほとんど**　*generally; mostly*

宿題がだいたい終わりました。　*My homework is mostly finished.*

Chapter 3

Degree (Negative)　なかなか・めったに・まったく・ちっとも ┈┈┈┈┈┈┈┈

■ **なかなか〜ない**　*hardly*
なかなか漢字が覚えられません。
I can hardly remember any kanji.

This is different from the positive expression なかなか いいね, which means *pretty good (but not perfect)*

■ **めったに〜ない**　*rarely*
めったに日本語を話しません。　*I rarely speak Japanese.*

■ **まったく〜ない**　*never*
運動をまったくしません。　*I never exercise at all.*

■ **ちっとも〜ない**　*not even a little*
あの人はちっとも私の言うことを聞きません。
That person doesn't listen to a single thing I say.

emphasizing feeling　まったく・ほんとうに・ぜひ・どうか・やはり・やっぱり

■ **まったく**　*completely; at all*

新しい仕事は、まったく違う種類の仕事です。
My new job is a completely different type of work.

まったく理解できない。
I can't understand it at all.

頭に来るね。
This drives me crazy.

まったくだよ。
I completely agree.

■ **本当に・ほんとに**　*truly; really*

UFOを本当に見たんです！
I really saw a UFO!

ほんと？
Truly?

■ **たしかに**　*for sure, definitely*

たしかにここに書類を置きました。　*I'm sure I left the documents here.*

■ **ぜひ**　*by all means, absolutely*

ぜひ家に来てください。　*By all means, please come by.*

ぜひ見てみたいです。　*I absolutely want to see that.*

■ **どうか**　*somehow*

どうか合格できますように！　*I hope I can somehow pass my exam!*

どうか許してください！　*Please forgive me somehow!*

■ **やはり・やっぱり** (formal/informal)　*as I thought; as expected*

日本の夏は暑いと聞いていたけど、やはり暑かったです。

I had heard that summers in Japan were hot, and as expected they were.

あの人、今婚活してるんだって。
They say she is looking for a husband now.

やっぱりね〜。
As I thought...

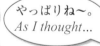

■ **もちろん**　*of course*

結婚式には、もちろん出席しますよ。

Of course, I will attend the wedding ceremony.

■ **〜はもちろん〜も**

This is an idiomatic phrase.

あの人は英語はもちろん、ドイツ語も話せるそうです。

That person speaks English of course, but apparently they can also speak German.

漢字はもちろん、カタカナも難しい。

Kanji is difficult of course, but so is katakana.

Adverbs formed from adjectives

i-adjectives　　　　い changes to く

　　はやい ➡ はやく走る。　　たのしい ➡ 友達とたのしく話した。

na-adjectives　　　add に

　　じょうず ➡ じょうずに話せる。　　きれい ➡ きれいにする。

Time　最近・このごろ・さっき・これから・これまで・そろそろ・一度に・ふと

■ **最近**　*these days; nowadays*
　　最近どうですか？　*How are you these days?*

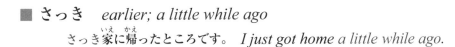

■ **このごろ**　*recently; lately*
　　このごろ元気がないですね。　*You've been down lately.*

■ **さっき**　*earlier; a little while ago*
　　さっき家に帰ったところです。　*I just got home a little while ago.*

■ **これまで**　*until now*
　　これまでうまくいってた。　*It was going well until now.*

■ **これから・今から**　*from now on*
　　これから（今から）そちらに行きますよ。　*I'm going to go there from now on.*

■ **そろそろ**　*soon; about time to*
　　そろそろ行かないといけません。　*I have to go soon.*

■ **一度に・いっぺんに**　*simultaneously; at once*
　　３つのプロジェクトを一度に（いっぺんに）しています。
　　I'm working on three projects at once.

■ **突然・いきなり**　*suddenly*
　　突然、雷が鳴り始めました。　*Suddenly, a peal of thunder rang out.*

■ **ふと**　*unintentionally; happen to do*
　　ふと、昔のことを思い出しました。
　　I unintentionally started thinking about the past.
　　ふと、後ろを見たら、友達が立っていた。
　　When I happened to look behind me, my friend was standing there.

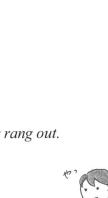

Common questions

Q There's so many styles of speech in Japanese and I don't know how to use them properly.

Let's break it down. Broadly, there's a speaking style and writing style, each of which have differing politeness levels.

✳ Speaking style

1. **Honorific (*keigo*)**: When speaking to bosses, customers, or people that you don't know well.
   これはお茶でございます。

2. **Polite (*teineigo*)**: For people of the same social standing as you or that you somewhat know.
   これはお茶です。

3. **Casual (*tameguchi*)**: Family, friends, and other people you know well.
   これ、お茶。　これ、お茶だよ。　お茶だね。

✳ Writing Style

1. Business emails, notes to superiors ➡ The same *keigo* as speaking style

2. Essays, letters to acquaintances ➡ The same *teineigo* as speaking style

3. Social-media posts ➡ The same *tameguchi* as speaking style

4. Reports and newspaper articles ➡ Written in plain form, but doesn't use particles like ね and よ.

   これはお茶だ。　これはお茶である。

◼ Style Comparisons

Honorific	Polite	Casual	Writing
Is it good? よろしいでしょうか？	いいですかね？	いいかな？	いいのだろうか？
They said it's good. いいとおっしゃいました。	いいと言いました。	いいって。	いいと言った。
Is that tomorrow? 明日でしたでしょうか？	明日でしたっけ？	明日だっけ？	明日だったろうか？

Q What's the differences between こと, もの and の?

Essentially, もの refers to tangible things while こと refers to intangible things.

大切_{たいせつ}なもの 　　　　　　　　大切_{たいせつ}なこと

大切_{たいせつ}なものはお金_{かね}です。　　大切_{たいせつ}なことは愛_{あい}です。

The thing I cherish is money.　　*The thing I cherish is love.*

You can substitute の for either of these.

➡ 大切_{たいせつ}なのはお金_{かね}です。　　大切_{たいせつ}なのは愛_{あい}です。

There is also the expression ものだ, which is used when remembering something that happened often in the past. The kanji for もの is not used in this case, and こと can't be substituted.

よく遊_{あそ}んだものだ。
I used to play a lot.

* Nominalizing a verb (converting it to a noun) is typically done with の, although こと is also used sometimes.

本を読_よむのがすきです。　　（読_よむことがすきです）
I like reading books.

* Information

事故_{じこ}があったことをしってます。➡ 事故_{じこ}があったのをしってます is also fine.
I know about the accident.

事故_{じこ}のことしってますか？　　➡ When no verb comes before こと, you can't use
Did you know about the accident?　の because that would make it のの.

あなたのことがすき。　　　　　➡ When こと is used, the phrase あなたが好_すき
I like everything about you.　　carries a deeper meaning.

* Explanations

準備中_{じゅんびちゅう} …… つまり、いまお店に入れないということです。 Can't use もの here.
"Preparing"...in other words, we can't enter the store right now.

* Sights and Sounds

女_{おんな}の人_{ひと}が立_たってるのがみえる。　　鳥_{とり}が鳴_ないてるのがきこえる。 Can't use こと here.
I see a woman standing there.　　*I hear a bird chirping.*

* Reasons

怒_{おこ}っているのは、心配_{しんぱい}だからです。 Can't use こと here.
The reason I'm angry is that I'm worried.

* Replacing Words

レッスンが始_{はじ}まるの（時間_{じかん}）は1時_{いちじ}です。 Can't use こと here.
The lesson start (time) is 1 o'clock.

Q よう has so many meanings. How can I use it properly?

The different usages of よう are explained on other pages, but here is a list that might make them easier to keep straight. Rather than trying to equate the various usages to English, you should try to memorize Japanese phrases that use each of them.

1. Showing the reason an action is done
   合格できるようにがんばります。 *I'll work hard so that I can pass.*

2. Making soft commands
   勉強するように！ *Make sure you study!*

3. Expressing hopes and prayers
   合格できますように。 *I hope I can pass.*

4. Gaining the ability to do something
   日本語が話せるようになりました。 *I became able to speak Japanese.*

5. Trying to do something habitually
   日本語を話すようにしています。 *I'm trying to speak Japanese.*

6. Indicating your next action
   野菜を食べようとしています。 *I'm about to eat some vegetables.*

7. Comparing a thing or action to something else
   彼は日本人のようです。 *He appears to be Japanese.*
   彼女はネイティブのように日本語を話します。 *She speaks Japanese like a native.*

8. Introducing some explanation
   前にお話ししたように *As I mentioned before*

To get yourself familiar with all of these usages of よう, try creating your own Japanese sentences using the examples above, then translate them to English.

Practical Japanese 3

2020年2月10日　第1刷発行
2024年1月16日　第2刷発行

著　者　小川 清美

発行者　浦　　晋亮

発行所　IBCパブリッシング株式会社
　　　　〒162-0804 東京都新宿区中里町29番3号 菱秀神楽坂ビル
　　　　Tel. 03-3513-4511 Fax. 03-3513-4512
　　　　www.ibcpub.co.jp

印刷所　株式会社シナノパブリッシングプレス

ISBN978-4-7946-0616-7

装幀: 斉藤啓（ブッダプロダクションズ）